The

THE OCCULT COMPENDIUM

Disclaimer: No part of this work may be reproduced, distributed, sold, replicated, or edited in any manner without the express written consent of the author. It may be reviewed or excerpted where credit is properly given.

TARL WARWICK

2015

The Occult Compendium

Introduction

"*Musings*" seeks to enlighten the reader in multiple ways. In its pages are contained passages which formerly represented a variety of essays and chapters from other works which I have written. These works, cobbled together as they were into one book, are nonetheless appropriately so, for the all follow the same basic line of reasoning.

Much as with "*Occult Philosophy for the Modern Age* "which I completed and released, the work focuses on the metaphysical, and in drawing connections between the spiritual world and various fields of human endeavor; politics, society, and so forth. In the present age, so often, the occult is regarded as entirely separate from other fields of experience- an oversight which could have been avoided by interpreting even the darkest grimoire as the steganography it almost invariably was.

The text you are holding right now was reformatted and re-edited from the original, which contained much the same content, albeit in a more poor choice of formats. Within it are explanations of the occult- a collection of

The Occult Compendium

observations regarding Satan and his nature, a collection of curses which maybe practiced (which are listed for academic purposes, of course,) and more- a topical covering of some rather pop culture materials as well, which nonetheless require explanation, and which are important within the occult.

Importantly, the occult is inseparable from all other fields; it represents them in their primordial state, and intertwines with them. I've observed before, that where science and the occult, or where any other academic or observational field and the mystic overlap, that is where some of the best wisdom is to be gleaned by both the occultist *and* the secular academic. A few people have realized this- even in the period of eugenics and theosophy this led to mass technological progress, as ancient ideas were realized as possible and were expounded upon. We get the same notion from the (largely false) notion of some islamic renaissance or muslim golden age; for the technology, philosophy, and works of pagans from centuries before, which had been regarded as heretical, were excavated from the ruins and put to use by alchemists and inventors. A great deal of social and technological progress was made, even though most of the works masqueraded as spiritual texts

The Occult Compendium

only. The return of pagan lore and pagan ideology to what had been a stark abrahamic hatred for all progress in turn modernized the latter and not many centuries later the world entered upon the Renaissance and for the first time since the height of Rome there existed stable cultures and those same groups were then capable of expanding once more- this time, across the Atlantic Ocean.

Importantly, I must state here; while this work contains what may be considered generally secular Satanic philosophy, I am no longer a Satanist, but have embraced paganism at this time. To me, Satan remains a powerful archetype of intelligence and liberation, and Satanism remains at least a good stepping stone to other fields, despite my belief that it is at most an introductory phase within the spiritual which should be forsaken once an individual has liberated themselves of false fear and guilt almost surely imparted to them by a church in their youth, as is almost invariably the case in the western world where one may think the Puritans still exist if they observe our laws.

The Occult Compendium

Table of Contents

I: The Five Forms of the Devil

II: Some simple Curses: An Academic Catalog

III: Refutation of Asceticism

IV: The Occult Ninth Gate

V: Creation in Sumeria

VI: The Psychic Arts

VII: The New Satanism

VIII: Occult Resources

The Occult Compendium

CHAPTER I

The Five Forms of the Devil

While the Devil has an inexhaustible number of forms to appear in, five major forms exist sufficient to describe most of its wanderings.

When we use the term "it" to describe the Devil, we of course are acknowledging that, as a sentient but often non-physical being, the Devil is fully capable of appearing male, female, disgendered, or in a sexless, nearly immaterial form. This is the power of the Devil.

THE FIRST FORM: LUCIFER

The first form of the Devil is that of the fallen angel. While "Lucifer" is of course not a proper noun and was never really meant to describe the Devil in a real sense (and is the result of medieval scholars not understanding how to translate Greek words) this does not prevent the Devil from using this form.

The Occult Compendium

Lucifer is anthropoid in appearance, often angelic, shining, radiant– Lucifer is the flame of Prometheus, the serpent of Eden, who tempts mankind to better itself by rebuking the tyranny of Jehovah, who liberates us from spiritual slavery.

Lucifer is the inner potency of the rebel spirit within mankind itself– an ancient knowledge that, in the face of propaganda from christians and muslims and jews, has retained its power but not its spread.

Lucifer is the question, Lucifer is there when you ask "why is it this way… why is the world filled with idiots…" Lucifer is the arbiter of freedom, the light that guided the enlightenment of secular society in its brief glory before it too was extinguished by fanatics.

THE SECOND FORM: SATAN

The second form of the Devil is that of the insufferably evil demon of Hell. Satan is the destroyer, but he does not destroy that which is good, but is employed to

The Occult Compendium

destroy the wicked and vile.

Satan is the fires of the forge which turns stone into ingots of gold, the perfecter of action, of mind, of spirit, the ultimate purifying cleansing.

Satan is the spirit of righteous warfare, the judgment of evil, the end to evil.

Satan is the action, Satan is there when you destroy that which is wrong, even when society believes it to be right, Satan is the divine revolutionary, the fighter for justice, the hammer smashing the skull of a tyrant, the bullet in the brain of a criminal, the vigilante that ignores convention and does what is right.

THE THIRD FORM: PAN

The third form of the Devil is the mischievous, sensual, sexual figure of Pan. Pan entertains, Pan teaches poetry, music, seduction, lust, romance, love… Pan is the dancer, the actor, the lover.

The Occult Compendium

Pan is the words of a poem that bring you to tears, Pan is beautiful music, Pan is the feared sexual drive that opposes the celibacy of the unworthy charlatans who pray to Jesus while they have sex with children.

Pan is the joke, the laugh, joy, freedom from struggle and want, the figure of the holiday and the feast.

Pan is there when you make love, when you enjoy yourself, the jovial, the cheerful, the glad.

THE FOURTH FORM: THE BEAST

The fourth form of the Devil is that of the beast, the ancient figure of nature. The beast is natural law, tooth and claw, struggle, and yet comfort in the knowledge of a natural existence which man is not yet free from nor ever will be.

The beast is the wind in the trees, crickets at night, the waves of the ocean, and the sun overhead, and the moon.

The Occult Compendium

The beast is there when you are in solitude, when you are in the forests, at sea, in the desert, when you are connected to the world and not to mankinds hideous cities.

THE FIFTH FORM: DEATH

The fifth form of the Devil is death, the end of life and the beginning of new life- the seed from a dead plant.

Death is ever present, and it is seen by the unwise as the end, or of a period of transformation, yet it is not- death is the frost that releases the seed back into the world so that new life can later emerge.

Death is the renewal of matter, the removal of detritus and the repurification of matter, the reproductive cycle itself is death and life.

Death is there when you reproduce, for all life must die and then be reborn- death is there of course when you die, when you are transmuted into decay and spring back into infancy yet anew. Death is the final judge of your

The Occult Compendium

physical state.

THE TRUE NATURE OF THE DEVIL

In truth, the Devil is all of these things and yet none of them.

True, the Devil has those five major archetypal forms, based on the flawed symbology of the human race, but the Devil is, essentially, that which is *feared yet desirable*.

The charlatans within the worlds churches thus attempt to control aspects of peoples lives, preventing them from being free like Satan, natural like the Beast, the church tries to block them from re-entering this paganistic cycle to enjoy life over and over again, by telling them what to do and not to do, to waste their lives praying to their eternally dead idols.

The church informs society, and visa versa, but now we can expose these five forms and why the church fears them.

The Occult Compendium

It fears the enlightenment of Lucifer, because if people improve their lives through secularism or science, religion is often thus seen as a greedy scam to make money (and it is.)

It fears the judgment of Satan, because if people rise up to rebuke the church for its own numerous shortcomings, the church will fall into ruins.

It fears the sensuality of Pan, because if people place their family and personal joy above the church, the church will be impotent to regulate their sexuality.

It fears the naturism of the Beast, because if people respect nature, they will see the churches as hideous and avoid them, because they are created from dead trees and rocks which looked better by the river before they were quarried.

It fears death most of all, because if people understood that death was just part of a renewing cycle, they would not fear it and would feel no reason to pay priests and pastors and rabbis and imams large sums to preach to them.

The Occult Compendium

The church is fear, religion is fear, the Devil is the ultimate arbiter of liberation from fear of death, and of life, at the same time.

The religious sheep in the church fear living almost more than they do dying because they have been taught that enjoying life is a bad thing, an amusing sort of nonsense that only fools truly believe- but they also have a fear of dying and this convinces the rest of them to go listen to a drunken priest rant for hours about sinning.

THE VARIOUS GOALS OF THE DEVIL

The Devil, the best friend mankind ever had, responsible for enlightening cultures, and inspiring social reform and the existence of the scientific method, is indeed possessed of the volition to have goals- something which is remarkably lost on most who acknowledge its existence, relegating the Devil to a sort of parlor sideshow, often talked about but seldom acknowledged as a real entity, which displeases the Devil greatly.

The Occult Compendium

The essential goal of the Devil is freedom, which makes sense given the typical archetype of the Devil as opposed to authority (which the church never bothers to mention was tyrannical.)

The presence of Lucifer frees you from guilt, from tyranny, from the error of not questioning things. It frees you from the lies of religion.

The presence of Satan frees you from the ill will of authority itself in a more physical sense. It smashes states and the iron heel of dictators and rulers.

The presence of Pan frees you from sadness and gloom. It invites pleasure and sensuality, it opposes drudgery and stasis.

The presence of the Beast frees you from artifice and artificial morals. It invites you to relax and unwind, it opposes the forces of society itself with its cardboard houses and tin can cars.

The presence of Death frees you from fear and

The Occult Compendium

cowardice, it shows you that you are eternal, th[at you should]
fear nothing because, regardless of your state of [being, you will]
emerge victorious. In its penultimate form it als[o frees you]
from death itself, since it reveals (to all willing to listen) that
it is not the end, that it bears you no torment or ill will, but
wishes for you to be renewed eternally.

PRAISING THE DEVIL

Seldom do people understand that they praise the Devil every day, and there is a secret here for all those who can understand these words, and that secret is as follows:

"The Devil does not care if you cast occult rituals around its presence, because simply understanding that the Devil is real, and is your friend, and governs all things good and sacred to the existence of life, is enough to reveal to you the divine truth: that every moment you express freedom or creativity, every time you enjoy yourself, you are vicariously becoming the Devil itself, and thus through these acts, inviting the Devil to share in your joy and freedom."

While you may certainly practice the occult and

The Occult Compendium

praise or evoke demons, summon various entities, curse your foes, bless your friends, and do any manner of things involving magick, the Devil itself is relatively unconcerned with such acts and is, essentially, the very spirit and existence of a sentient beings capability to enjoy itself- a capability maximized by the presence of freedom from authority, freedom from want, freedom from stasis, and from fear.

So here is the ultimate blasphemy (blasphemy properly understood as opposing church dogma rather than opposing "things that are good or holy") that the Devil is the guiding hand behind all fruitful and wholesome human endeavors.

The Devil is within you and without you, allowing you to do whatever you choose to do, and trying to show you that this is the way to exist in happiness.

Fear of need is a form of need itself, fear of death is a form of death itself, these are things the mundane minds of the confused are not able to understand.

Mankind exists in a perpetual state of struggle- between the forces of slavery and death (easily and most well

The Occult Compendium

personified by any organized religion) and the forces of liberation and continuous life (personified by the Devil.)

It is no small source of amusement that the very word "Lucifer" which every priest fears to the bone is actually used to refer to Jesus at one point in the new testament, for if they understood the truth of the Devil, these priests would realize that the teachings of this being are actually comparable to those of Jesus insofar as the possibly mythical figure of Jesus wandered the natural world like a beast, spurned authority, and didn't care whether he lived or died.

That the ultimate heresy is just this– that the worship of the Devil is not inverted god worship, but that god worship is an inverted form of worshiping the spirit of the Devil itself, a perfected being which brings nothing but truth, light, and knowledge to mankind, embracing humans, for some undetermined reason, as its fellow citizens in this vast existence.

SATAN LOVES YOU, THE CHURCH HATES YOU

The charlatans in any church, who exist because they

The Occult Compendium

con people out of their money in exchange for useless services and prayers to a demonic and malevolent being, pretend to understand sacred truth while feeding their jaded followers only the most virulent and poisonous of lies.

That these arrrogant individuals are trusted and seen as blessed is astounding... that they are taken seriously is alarming... that they are obeyed is disgusting- for what did a priest do for anyone other than convince them they were dirty, fallen, terrible, that their life was forfeit unless they existed in perpetual fear of punishment?

No better comparison exists than of an abusive man who beats his wife while telling her that he loves her- what pious christian would respect such a reprehensible individual?

They excuse their dead god by claiming he has eternal authority- the same authority claimed by the psychopathic abusive husband or the serial killer whose only concern is that his warped mind be put at ease by the presence of fresh blood- a tyrant god of no redeeming value.

One amusing side note- that the first groups (the

The Occult Compendium

gnostics) that realized this god was a tyrant were themselves tyranically butchered systematically by the catholics at the behest of the first christian emperor (Constantine) who himself butchered tens of thousands of people in order to steal power in Rome.

The Devil is not like this- for the Devil, as realized by the secular founders of western civilization, and by the gnostic wise men, and by millions of people today, is good, and the god of the hebrews, is an insane, greedy pig deserving nothing but a boot in his face for eternity.

You now know the truth, go forth in good measure, and propagate it whereveer the seeds of truth may be properly sown and bear fruit.

The Occult Compendium

CHAPTER II

Some Simple Curses: An Academic Catalog

Within this short section are expounded some historically important, basic curses. They are not provided here for actual curse work, but rather instead for the amusement of the reader. This is, basically, an excerpt of material from various backgrounds- Hoodoo, Greek, and Appalachian. These three areas alone contain collectively thousands or tens of thousands of texts on the subject matter and the reader can find and explore them at their leisure.

A SIMPLE HOODOO CURSE

This ritual will involve coffin nails and grave dirt, as well as an image of your enemy (which is likely a living person.)

You will need to bury the image of your enemy in the earth, in whatever location you may find suitable, mixing the grave dirt and nails in with their image (photograph, etc) and perform a very short invocation of

The Occult Compendium

sorts over the matter.

> May my enemy be destroyed
> Sickness come
> Darkness come
> Evil magick fill their life
> All evil spirits fill them
> All evil spirits harm them
> Until these nails are on their own coffin
> Until this dirt is dirt which surrounds their body

You will repeat this recitation three times (three often being an important number.) Over the coming weeks or months, your enemy may very well fall ill, lose some sort of noble title they have gained, or perhaps their love life will fall to shit. This is the purpose of your spell.

If at some point you become satisfied that they have suffered enough, and you wish to banish these destructive forces, you will need to dig up the image of them (you may leave the nails and dirt behind wherever they were to begin with) and place the image amongst a small amount of salt, then perform a different invocation.

The Occult Compendium

> My revenge is had
> Go, evil spirits, back to the darkness
> Go, evil spirits, trouble no more
> You have done your task
> I command it!

At this point the spirits will depart, as they have performed the task you set out to accomplish. You may choose to leave out money or some other offering to them, lest any linger and in turn bring harm to you wherever you may be.

ANOTHER HOODOO RITUAL TO HARM A FOE

For this ritual you will need to obtain a small amount of salt- you will form this into a small circle upon a table of sorts (or an altar if you have one) and surround a black candle with it. You will burn one black feather (from a crow or raven) upon the candle flame as you recite the following, after which you will also burn an image of your enemy on the same candle flame, letting it burn itself out afterward.

The Occult Compendium

As the crow flies above the graves
As the raven feasts upon the dead
Spirits of evil go to my enemy
Suck the life from them!

Let them get sick
Their lungs grow weary
Exhaust their energy
The manifestation of old age and weariness

Go enemy
Trouble me no more!
Trouble me not!
Psychopomp go forth!

Once the feather and image are burnt the spell is in work actively– you may banish these same forces through an exceedingly simple process– produce an identical image of the enemy and leave it covered in salt upon the same table or altar overnight, during which period you again recite a banishing as follows:

My enemy is defeated

The Occult Compendium

Go away evil spirits
Go back to the shadows
Trouble nobody
Begone!

TRIANGULATION RITUALS

In some ancient cultures (especially Greece.) they made amulets or pottery/wax tablets upon which were written triangular recitations which were meant to bring harm to a foe (among a multitude of other possible uses.) This fits in very roughly with the idea of sacred geometry.

Here are a few things which may be inscribed upon a sheet of paper which has been made roughly triangular. Write your enemies' name wherever "N." appears, then store the paper away as you would a sigil and burn it when its effects have been well documented and completed. You may also inscribe these on wax or clay and store them, or make them into amulets.

N. has troubled me, let them trouble me no more, may they infest the grave

The Occult Compendium

Let them wander around confused and find no shelter like a hermit
Let them find that their friends have abandoned them
Let them sicken or die
It is done

N. is a most revolting human being, let this be known to all people
Their trust dissolve so that they may be lonely
Their body grow weak and sick
It is done

In the name of Zeus, N. has been stirring up trouble within my life
Judge me worthy oh gods, to call upon your power
That N. may suffer for this indignity
For they disrespect my ways
It is done

The wicked ways of N. make life a daily struggle to cope
Oh ancient ones hear this plea to your power now
That N. may be destroyed and wither away

The Occult Compendium

That N. may falter and be subsumed
It is done

GREEK STYLE INCANTATIONS

The Greeks had a method of healing sickness with a simple three line, thrice repeated linguistic method. It followed roughly this pattern:

I have a problem
What problem do I have?
I have no problem

This method can be altered slightly to bring about destruction upon an enemy- a few suggestions follow, where "N." is the name of an enemy or, perhaps, a place. This simple reversal takes advantage of essentially the very same force that the wise and powerful Greeks used to heal. You should repeat each one three times to use its full force.

N. is not sick
How is N. sick?

The Occult Compendium

N. has cancer

N. is wealthy and prosperous
Is N. wealthy and prosperous?
N. is rather poor and wretched

N. is popular
Is N. popular?
N. is not popular

The possibilities of this language reversal are endless. When you wish for the power to be banished from use, there is one particular incantation of this kind that you may use.

I have cursed N.
How have I cursed N?
I have lifted the curse from N.

ANOTHER GREEK METHOD TO CURSE

This method of cursing an enemy works very well in

The Occult Compendium

my experience, and requires rather limited effort if you can locate a graveyard in which one of your enemies' ancestors has been buried.

You must first locate a grave containing such an ancestor if possible (in some cases this may not be possible at all in which case the ritual cannot be performed.) Simply place a single white candle upon the gravestone (if it is round, place it in front of the gravestone above where the body will be located) and perform the following incantation to bring the wrath of the spirit upon them. This will not work with a non-related corpse as there would be no reason for the spirit to be angry and trouble them.

> Spirit awake!
> Your relative has been quite troubling
> Did you envision your family line ending with such antics?
> Did you envision your blood acting so?
> Did you envision your kin behaving so rudely?
>
> You know who they are
> Their ways will quickly be the downfall of your lineage

The Occult Compendium

Go now, forth, from the grave
Trouble them
Haunt them

Change their ways, oh spirit
Until they reform their behavior
And apologize for all wrongdoing
Or, if they will not change their ways
Then bring them sickness in a further attempt to change them

And if they still not change
May you bring down your full anger upon them

Go forth now!

After the ritual you may extinguish the candle and leave a small offering to the spirit for the benefit of their lineage- some sort of goods representing good fortune so that they will know your quarrel is not with their family but merely with one individual from their family.

The Occult Compendium

HORSESHOE MAGICK

This magick comes from my own area of the world in New England– I have seen my mother use it, and around here, barns almost always have a lucky horseshoe placed upon the front, right above the door (sometimes on the inside, sometimes outside.) The idea is that the horseshoe, facing upwards, is holding luck inside it, while if it somehow finds itself pointing downwards, the luck is draining and turning to bad luck.

There are several methods by which a horseshoe can be used to curse one of your enemies– they all require a literal metal horseshoe, a picture or facsimile of one will not work.

The first possibility; you bury a horseshoe, upside down (open side downward) somewhere on their property. This will not be possible, most of the time, in an urban area, or for example if your enemy lives in an apartment complex (although you could curse the entire building by putting it at the corner of the property outside the complex.)

The Occult Compendium

You can also, if there are trees on their property, nail a horseshoe upside down on one of them, although the likelihood that they will see the horseshoe and remove it is possible (in New England if you were discovered doing this, it would be quite a blow to your local reputation as most people would know what its purpose was.)

A horseshoe placed under their doormat, or near their door, leaning against a wall facing downwards works just as well- in fact it can essentially be placed anywhere so long as it is in or near their home or apartment, and upended so that the spirit of luck drains from it forming a sort of small "black hole of luck."

To reverse the curse simply remove the horseshoe- and of course a horseshoe placed the normal way on their property will increase fortune.

THE PENNY CURSE

I am not sure what culture this comes from but I know it is used in Florida and in the deep south so I imagine

The Occult Compendium

it is creole in origin. A penny is nailed to the wall, over an image of your enemy- and the setup removed once the enemy has been thwarted. Old, copper pennies or other copper coins are useful for this work, but modern zinc pennies give mixed results: copper is seen as useful within alchemy particularly for energy direction while zinc is not, so this may be the cause.

Other coins also don't seem to work, and old pennies are fairly easy to obtain so this is a cheap, reliable method to curse.

CHINESE PENNY CURSE

In Asian circles, particularly in Chinese culture, placing four pennies under the doormat or near the door of another residence is used as a curse method.

This cheap and effective curse is often combined with the use of rice and cooking oil (or so it is said) and it does seem to work- you can simply soak the rice in cooking oil and scatter them around the four pennies, under your enemies' doormat, or nearby.

The Occult Compendium

    The pennies should be placed upside-down, if they are placed facing upwards it does not curse your enemy, but rather is supposed to give them good luck- it is not necessary to actually use chinese pennies for this purpose, any pennies will do.

BLACK CANDLE (CONSECRATION CURSE)

    With this simplistic pagan-style hex you will be consecrating a black candle through invocation, and subsequently you will simply burn an image of your enemy upon it.

    Obtain a black candle, and place it upon a small amount of grave dirt (dirt from around a tombstone in a cemetery- check your local ordinances as it may be legal or illegal to harvest in your area.) Then, recite as follows:

> May this black candle hold all of my malice
> Negative energy only, enter into its flame
> To consume and feed upon an image of the one to

The Occult Compendium

destroy
That they may be deeply troubled

As the potency of the spinning wheels of the black
sun
Devour the enemy upon every side
So to, this candle, symbol of this power
Feast upon my foes remains

Fires of Hela, the rays of the moon betwixt the
flames
Inferno to subsume the hate of my enemy

It is done!

Now, simply use this candle to burn up an image of one single foe- the candle can be any style as long as it is consecrated for ritual use- it is extremely simple and candle-work is often used for curse purposes.

The Occult Compendium

SUMMONING A HUNGRY GHOST TO FEED ON YOUR FOE

In Buddhist tradition, a hungry ghost is a sort of wretched being of constant hunger, which normally resides in a desolate underworld, unable to satiate its own hunger due to a tiny mouth shaped like a straw- but these beings (which are even lower in the Buddhist hierarchy than demons) do attempt to feed upon beings in this physical realm from time to time, and will hardly reject an invitation to feed upon your enemy in any way they can. Their abilities are limited but it's possible such an invocation will attract not one but several of these beings to the marked, cursed individual, amplifying any effects.

Simply recite as follows, while gazing upon an image of your enemy- if you are able to enter a meditative state, and focus utterly upon it, so much the better. "N." is replaced with your foes name.

> Into the realm of the underworld I channel this command and call
> May the hungering, slavering beings thereof, plague

The Occult Compendium

N.

From the North, come and feed
From the South, to dance about, feasting
From the East, gleeful as you sap their life
From the West, creep upon them

This life is yours for the taking
Bleed N. dry of their laughter
Until they too hunger and lust for sustenance
Gluttony overtake them
Impart to them your hungering nature

As you were cast low for your crimes
Now, a short reprieve, as you feed upon N.
To ascend once again through the hierarchies
Alleviate now your hunger

It is done!

CHAPTER III

Refutation of Asceticism

INTRODUCTION

Asceticism, literally a lifestyle of abstaining from "worldly pleasures" has been dominant in certain subsets of occultism and theosophy for centuries- the going principle of asceticism even extends to forms of magickal work which do not have relation to the same eastern sources where the practice is most common (Buddhism, Hinduism, or the Orthodox hesychasists.)

Many are the occult or philosophical writings which praise the practice of abstinence, often revolving around the notion (in both ancient and modern sources) of purifying oneself before contact with entities, performing invocations, and so forth- but where is the philosophy of totality? Where is the regard for the very physical? For the mind itself- a wondrous organ- is a physical tool to the occultist- a beacon for the astral, and a connection to the worlds above.

The Occult Compendium

Refuting asceticism is fairly simple- for the dogmatic principles which dominate its use are entirely idiotic, with its adherents proclaiming that all sensual pleasures are a form of egoism, often while at the same time becoming egotistical themselves, haughty in their supposedly superior lifestyle.

Nor are the hesychasists doing themselves a favor when they practice quite effective invocations while mixing and matching religious principles from eastern sources which have entirely different meanings.

As the monks of Buddhism and Christianity in the world cloister themselves away behind thick stone walls, eating their whole grain breads and wearing their simple robes, they are stating, to the entire world, effectively the following.

"I am not able to live a moral, spiritual life amongst other people because I am weak to temptation, and I am a slave to the carnal- thus rather than improve myself day by day and face the world around me, and attempt to be spiritual, I surround myself with masochistic abstinence so that I can dull my pleasure centers into oblivion."

The Occult Compendium

In essence, the same folks which are regarded as the most pure in spirit, holy, and high, are effectively the least spiritual, for they often have left the physical world for that of a monastery precisely because they are not capable of remaining "morally intact" among us "mere mortals."

This is not to say that abstinence and other spiritual practices are not valid or meaningful, but that these particular ascetic individuals have removed themselves from all hope of a spiritual existence by essentially doing the exact opposite of the sheep who make up the bulk of society- they are not able to enjoy life, and will not enjoy the hereafter, but doom themselves to perpetual mental servitude.

FEARFUL ABSTINENCE FROM DRUGS IS DIRECTLY ANTITHETICAL TO TRUE SPIRITUALITY

Perhaps the single most antispiritual practice among the ascetics is their twofold, false argument (among most ascetic groups) against the consumption of mind altering substances.

The Occult Compendium

They first argue, that these substances cause sensual pleasure and are thus not to be condoned- an argument which is in itself based on, perhaps, a slow seeping of establishment-based western views into eastern circles which in ancient times seem not to have considered such substances to be incompatible with a spiritual life.

They also argue that they distract the mind from focused spiritual practices (read: meditation or yoga or hesychasm.) This argument is even more inspired by lunacy- how can they forget that their ancestors only invented organized religion in the first place because they were hallucinating after ingesting mushrooms or seeds?

In reality, the modern ascetic movement is directly antithetical to the authentic ancient spiritualities- and here let us give a few examples.

Of the Sumerians which directly influenced judaism- and their veneration of the god Enki which seems to have fed Adamu (or Adam) hallucinogenics so that he would stop crouching in the bushes like an ape, enslaved to tyrants.

The Occult Compendium

Of the tantric Buddhists, some schools of which do not believe mind altering substances to be of a negative nature unless they are causing addiction or routinely interfering with higher mental or physical functions. (These particular Buddhists are among the only ones with a realistic view of life- we will revisit them later on the topic of sexuality and spirutuality.)

Of the early Christians which seem to have ingested various drugs to connect with Jehovah- a practice that seems to have culminated in the late middle ages with various religious art depicting mushrooms and other drugs- anyone who has seen the great artwork of Heironymous Bosch understands these individuals- all of whom were Christians- were regularly ingesting *some* entheogens.

While abstaining from drugs (particularly in the case where the individual is not able to ingest them without negative effects, or is very young) is sometimes very much appropriate, the ascetics frown upon them for no other purpose than some monk or scribe said they were bad. Western practitioners of Eastern religious practices further degrade themselves by listening to law enforcement or the media in such matters.

The very birth of spirituality seems, in the anthropological record, to coincide directly with the rise of the use of mind altering substances- even today this process continues, with mushroom cults cropping up occasionally in some jungle or desert where the practitioners commune with their gods.

ABSTINENCE FROM SEXUALITY IS ALSO ANTISPIRITUAL

Abstaining from all sexuality is further degrading to a spiritual lifestyle- again as we stated before, it is in both the spiritual as well as the physical that liberation of the self occurs.

Some early Christians used to have orgies- a practice which was natural to them as part of formerly pagan Rome- and why shouldn't they? After all, Rome stole the cult and made it its own- pumping it full of pagan ideals that were later accepted as Christian in nature- why not add rampant sexuality to the mix?

The Occult Compendium

But no! Said the Catholics, as they rubbed their greedy hands together and remarked to themselves "now we will show them that we even control their sexual organs" as they passed a slew of regulations which were scarcely even part of the original practice.

Interestingly the protestants (a bastardized Catholic branch) and the Catholics themselves, both frown upon extramarital relationships when, if one reads the bible, their savior himself says nothing on the subject- but these folks are truly best called Paulites and don't seem to care.

The Eastern groups which practice sexual abstinence are even more confused- for the authentic first Buddhists used to practice orgiastic rituals as well, while drunk and on drugs- this was seen as part of their spiritual system until much later when the practice was pressured to go underground in the face of colonialism, with all of its Judeochristian nonsense. Again however, the tantrics seem to have partly resisted this pressure, and accept sexuality as a genuinely spiritual practice in and of itself.

In reality these organized groups seem to have

spawned sexual ascetism not out of a desire to actually help their membership achieve enlightenment, or godhood, or paradise, but for (ironically) very worldly reasons- to control the breeding patterns of their laity and to regulate their sexual behaviors for, as any decent propagandist will admit, controlling the sexuality of a population makes them infinitely more easy to manipulate.

Sexuality is best seen as a spiritual practice in and of itself- not even one of an occult nature, but simply part of the creation process itself, and, from a more humanistic viewpoint, a proper way for homo sapiens to behave- as we observe all other animals above primitive eukaryotic life forms, and see them nearly indiscriminately mating, often for pleasure (as among the often homosexual Bonobo apes which may be a closer ancestor even than Chimpanzees) rather than any particular desire to even procreate.

ABSTINENCE FROM FOOD IS AS BAD AS OVERINDULGENCE

From a purely biological, functional viewpoint, abstaining from food and drink itself for any great period of

The Occult Compendium

time is hazardous, while shorter periods of abstinence thereof may be beneficial- there are instances where supposedly spiritual individuals have starved themselves for such a period of time that they die- which goes to show their fanaticism is no more positive than any fiery stump preacher.

And here we see a rather amusing spectacle- the dichotomous state of a skeleton-like monk meditating upon a cliff while meditating, and a nearly obese protestant minister delivering a sermon about how gluttony is a sin. These two individuals are both deceived.

Realistically speaking, the same monks and other assorted ascetics which will teach about abstaining from food also endorse a practice of mental neutrality and immovability- that they are not affected by outside stimuli and resist reactionary tendencies.

But this is folly- for their abstinence is indeed a form of stimuli itself, where they react to the stimulus of their own belief system, and find themselves unable to indulge. Here, yet again, we see the overall superiority of the tantric over other paths of a similar nature; for while the ascetic may beat themselves due to overeating (a lapse in spirituality their

The Occult Compendium

path despises) a tantric understands that, at times, it is important to deliberately shun your own spiritual path just to prove you have the willpower and capability to do so.

By falling into a routine of unbending asceticism, the ascetic has proven to the world that they are as weak willed and inflexible as any entirely hylic, physically obsessed sex addict or overeater- they have lost the capability of indulging the physical- a hypocritical state wherein they scrutinize others for being unable to indulge the spiritual.

The hypocrisy of the ascetic knows little in the way of boundary- for these individuals are often the most egotistical, unbending, and corrupt of all, with certain individuals proclaiming themselves reincarnated masters or demigods (especially in Hindu culture) and then selling their services, or promising to gather folks together to levitate or witness some other miracle, that then never manifests.

These have, in some cases, also spawned allegations of sexual abuse by these so-called masters or gurus, who proclaim the ascetic lifestyle while at the same time raping the laypeople physically or mentally, living a lavish lifestyle surrounded by crowns and thrones, and generally

The Occult Compendium

bastardizing the same principles they preach.

THE CATHOLIC QUESTION

Perhaps the most insane of all asceticism is the Catholic priest- with his supposedly high moral standards and unwavering obedience to Jehovah.

Anyone who has paid attention to events is aware that the priests have been raping children, and that the bishops, who ought to have excommunicated them or otherwise punished them, have stood by complacently and done nothing, in some cases even encouraging such behavior by shipping such pedophiles from parish to parish under the radar to protect the honor of the church (which is so tarnished it is barely worth protecting.)

Most of the laypeople understand the cause- the church has a threefold problem which accounts for the massive pedophilia and rape created in their organization.

Firstly, they disallow marriage and sex for priests, giving them no proper sexual outlet- just as when the

The Occult Compendium

government banned alcohol, alcoholism rose, so too did sexual abuse by priests become a problem solely because these individuals are expected to do the impossible- become completely asexual while surrounded by available sexual partners of all ages which look to them as just a few steps short of godhood.

Secondly, through trusting priests with both the secular and religious education of children in Catholic schools, the priests are constantly surrounded by a herd of virginal preteen children.

Thirdly, the church has taught that such authority figures are above question- that to question the validity of a priests behavior is in essence to question the validity of the religion itself which places such individuals in authoritative positions- the atmosphere of immutability thus feeds the priests ego and prevents the abused from coming forwards- and the wolves among the sheep in the church use this to full advantage.

So here we see the fruits of one of the most ascetic lifestyles available to a human being (that of a priest.) Rather than allow these individuals to practice the spiritual, it is a

The Occult Compendium

controlling, limited path which encourages their corruption and destroys lives.

THE BASTARD POPE RATZINGER

Of course it would be remiss not to mention the head of the Catholic hierarchy as a major cause of asceticism and thus corruption in the world today.

The pope; a former Nazi youth and formerly head of a group of officials which the former pope John Paul elected to the position of overseeing the 1990s era sex abuse allegations, has spent his happy, white-haired existence of late in the massive halls of the Vatican, wandering the grounds and thinking of new ways to tarnish his own reputation.

Here he has offered the typical Catholic solution to combining asceticism with realistic, physical existence– an ancient medieval practice called "the indulgence;" essentially paying off the church to avoid perdition as a result of having sinned. This way, the clergy and laypeople can sin, as long as they give more at the offering plate– how well this works for

The Occult Compendium

both parties!

Even the things which this organization considers evil are properly labeled normal, even blessed behavior: Anyone who has studied even a few authentic spiritual paths knows that, to the enlightened Greek or Roman ancients, there was absolutely no stigma at all associated with premarital sex, masturbation, orgies, group sex, bestiality, drug use, or almost anything else which is now frowned upon.

The Pope in Rome has his own problems- while trying to live this style of ascetic life he is surrounded by gold, crystal glass, fine wines, and streets paved with only the most expensive bricks money can buy in the slave-labor driven markets of Southeastern Asia- how difficult it must be for the pope, who sits upon his throne of gold and precious gems as he preaches that overindulging upon riches is a sin! This difficulty extends also to the bishops, none of whom seem to be impoverished like their savior was, first working as a low wage carpenter and subsequently taking up an entirely hermetic, migrant lifestyle- for although Jesus may be pictured as a well groomed man in a white robe with light coming out of his head, history tells us he was likely a

The Occult Compendium

scraggly-bearded hermit with a dirty sackcloth robe who squatted in the bushes beside the road as he strained to relieve himself of dysentery he got from bathing in the river.

Even Jesus, the (possibly mythical) savior of the world, had a tendency to demand folks give him their upper room for feasting with his disciples- where he partook in wine (a mind altering substance which some Christian ascetics ban.)

Muhammad tells us another interesting Ascetic story- for while alcohol and premarital sex are also banned in Islam, Muhammad tells that paradise is scattered with rivers of wine, and populated by perpetually virginal preteen boys (mentioned in such a way that it suggest homosexual relations with them are blessed) and multiple perpetually virgin wives for the faithful- a religion which of course offers female members little benefit, seeing them more as cattle or mobile sexual objects than actual human beings despite the best propagandist efforts of Middle Eastern oil barons to depict women as blessed in Islam.

The Occult Compendium

THE HYPOCRISY OF ASCETIC EGOTISM

The hypocritical manner in which some supposed ascetics voice themselves to the world is both annoying and hateful- and this is no more evident than among the Eastern Christians who have a fetish for the monastery and for monks.

Particularly when arguing the validity of their faith on the internet, they come off as both uneducated and simplistic- stating the defective nature of mans technology while using a computer. This extends to their sarcastic remarks about other religious groups (particularly atheists or agnostics) where you will notice them laughing heartily while simultaneously arguing that laughter and happiness are sensual and thus negative in nature.

I have also seen ascetics brag egotistically about, say, how enlightened they are (IE "I am so far above your understanding.") While some more traditionalist ascetics (the kind that you will rarely encounter outside of a Buddhist monastery) would argue that this is proof these individuals are not actually ascetics, it is fairly clear to see that they are-

The Occult Compendium

and merely practice a form of activist asceticism which more ancient Eastern sources would not necessarily agree with.

And here we have the ultimate hypocrisy of both asceticism and other religious, organized efforts- the belief that their way is so perfect, so blessed, and so correct, that they feel the need to shout it from the rooftops, and use their numbers to undermine facets of life for those who are from other groups- and while the squeaky wheel gets the oil and not all ascetics do so, those that choose this activist path are among the most violent and bigoted of human beings you can possibly have the misfortune of meeting.

Even more hysterical it is, when you meet a practitioner of the ascetic, who is new to their movement and who still reacts to physical stimuli- it is with glee that you may provoke them into a frenzy by suggesting they have any sort of incapability or disorder- they have not yet learned to completely ignore others, following their egotistical path.

You will note, as I have said, only individuals with massive ego problems, and either low self esteem or an excessive amount thereof, seem led to the ascetic lifestyle-

The Occult Compendium

ric or hesychasist may understand there is
 ad, most ascetics seem oblivious to this fact
 at they will reincarnate as gods if they go for
weeks without talking, eating, or farting- a goofy belief
system that essentially relegates their very existence to
meaninglessness as they have no capability to enjoy it.

THE BETTER PATH

The pure and simple fact is thus: That those who
gather themselves away from the world in communal
monasteries, and shun all things of a physical nature, are the
least rather than *most* spiritual- they are not capable of living
in either the world of dichotomy or the realm beyond
dichotomy- and are just as unable to indulge the physical as
most people are to indulge the truly spiritual.

Rather, the proper way to exercise the spiritual is as
follows: It is neither in the presence or absence of the flesh,
neither in the presence or absence of the spiritual, that actual
enlightenment, spiritual potency, and balance is created- and
those which follow either singular path (the ascetic or the
hylic) without regard to the other, cannot be spiritual

The Occult Compendium

entities.

If you are able to practice the spiritual, to abstain by choice, for smaller lengths of time, you more closely approach true spirituality than someone who lives in a cave in Tibet and sleeps on a flat rock so that they won't enjoy napping. It is far more impressive when an individual is able to meditate in a crowded place than when they meditate amongst bushes and vines.

You will not hear an ascetic admit this though- they will tell you that the physical world is fallen and terrible, oh woe are the masses for watching television and using money- but simply ask them, what has ascetism done for the world? Has it healed a disease? (In a verifiable manner, not some trumped up anecdotal way or in the pages of a 500 year old scripture.) Has it developed a vaccine? Has it invented anything useful that makes life easier?

Of course not- it is the same charade of phony spirituality that is dichotomously encompassed by western groups which revolve around external saviors or angels for communing with the spiritual- a nasty, diseased path which harms what it touches as much as the hylic does.

CHAPTER IV

The Occult Ninth Gate

INTRODUCTION

Ninth Gate is more than just an underrated and forgotten Polanski film- while critics cut it to pieces as "too artistic" or "slow paced" a few people came to the understanding that it was more than just a standard Hollywood film.

Best seen, perhaps, as occult in its own right, while the movie itself depicts fictional events, one ought to remember that the creator of this film has had his own run-ins with the occult, from his former wife, Sharon Tate, dabbling with white witchcraft, to the acid soaked sixties in the purest form, where Hollywood was entertained by only the most spooky of mysticism, from tarot and astrology to, of course, more demonic acts. *Rosemarys Baby* is, I suppose, another good example where the lines between physical reality and the supernatural are blurred.

The Occult Compendium

Through examining the reactions of several of the key characters within the film we begin to see a pattern emerge- a pattern escaped the observation of the critics and the public who consumed the material- those of us who have actually studied the occult in detail, however, may be led to different conclusions.

THE ARCHETYPAL CHARACTERS

Chief among the occult connections that can be derived from the film- the almost uncanny archetypes which we observe among several characters in regards to their own obsessions with the occult, and in particular with the Book of the Nine Gates of the Kingdom of Shadows.

Firstly, Boris Balkan (Frank Langella,) a rabid collector, a theistic believer in the Devil as a very real, corporeal entity- through contact with dark forces, he hopes to achieve power and control in the physical world.

Secondly, Baroness Kessler (Barbara Jefford,) also a rabid collector, a romanticist figure who believes in a very

The Occult Compendium

real Devil, however her reasons for studying and venerating this figure, are more related to her almost love-like feelings towards the Devil (as she admits, stating "I saw him (the Devil) once, I saw him as plainly as I see you now... it was love at first sight.")

Third, Bernie (James Russo) whose reaction to the books engravings ("Sensational, absolutely sensational...") shows his love for the material, but not for any high purpose, merely because it is old, rare, unique.

Fourth, Victor Fargas (Jack Taylor) the last member of a dying wealthy family, with a dwindling but still large collection, who treasures his own copy, and whose obsession with occult texts seems rooted primarily in his longing for younger, better days.

Fifth, Liana Telfer (Lena Olin) an extremely wealthy young woman whose copy seems primarily used to gather those in high society to her side with the promise of success and sex.

Of course, Dean Corso (Johnny Depp) forms the last character involved with this archetyping process- a sly,

The Occult Compendium

cunning agent who (from shots inside his apartment) seems to collect books, but is himself not a collector, merely the man collectors go to to obtain rare texts, but who ends up obsessed with the topic anyways.

These characters form a sort of archetypal structure around which the occult tenets of the story revolve.

THE ARCHETYPES EXPLAINED

Balkan is the archetype of those within the occult who, obsessed with its content, obsessed with the idea of power, will do anything (however morally ambiguous) to obtain more of its cherished teachings- indeed this character may even be a statement about the Satanic Panic, retrospectively summing up the view of Devil Worshipers of the time period, a period of time in which Charles Manson (a figure Polanski is certainly familiar with) was heavily featured in Hollywood and media stories about the supposed plague of Satan Worshiping miscreants sweeping the nation and killing children.

Kessler is the archetype of those within the occult

The Occult Compendium

who are not themselves practicing, but hold a sort of romantic vision of the Devil (or demonic forces) as interesting, good, or positive- a sort of romantic period Lord Byron view of Lucifer as a decent, good being with designs to liberate himself and humanity from the hold of a tyrannical deity named Jehovah- this archetype could also describe those who are drawn to the occult not by a desire to actually practice it, but out of pure curiosity (and these people are in the real world, quite numerous.)

Bernie is the archetype of those within the occult who collect, hoard, purchase occult materials, primarily for materialistic gain. Indeed, anyone who has casually glanced through book searches on ebay for occult material knows that, because so many occult authors use small publishers (which typically release hardcover only materials) and because so many booklet printings of shorter works command high prices, a person would be a fool to start collecting occult texts in the first place without having significant capital or extremely good sense of value. These individuals collect such materials, primarily because they stand to make a mint if they do it correctly.

Victor Fargas is the archetype of those within the

The Occult Compendium

occult who look to it as a sort of golden age material set- those who long for the days of old (either the victorian era with its early theosophy or the pre-medieval pagan era with its rife magickal usage- it isn't clear which one) who glorify it because, to them, it is something beautiful and, in a sort of double entendre, "magical."

Liana Telfer is the archetype of those within the occult who admire and use its ritualistic trappings primarily to obtain favor with those who they can influence through convincing others they have supernatural connections. I can think of no better example than Anton LaVey and the Church of Satan- an entirely atheistic organization that nonetheless has drawn great attention whenever they perform public rituals. That the dress and ritualism described in the film regarding Telfer and the sort of coven she leads, seems eerily familiar to LaVey's services in San Francisco in the 1960s, is remarkable. (Also of interesting note- that Susan Atkins, who had a hand in the slaying of Polanskis former wife Sharon Tate, performed at Church of Satan gatherings on several occasions!)

Dean Corso of course is of great concern- for his views towards the occult seem to shift over the course of the

The Occult Compendium

film as he interacts with others and encounters situations which are not easily explained by simple physical phenomena.

Corso may be thought of as the Devil himself- rising above law and authority, destroying all opposition, and finding liberation at the end of the movie, when the Ninth Gate is opened, and his quest is finished. He may also be thought of as the archetype of those who genuinely, truly practice the reality of occultism- it could even be a reference to pure mysticism as the proverbial *left hand path* in which the sacred feminine is venerated to achieve occult superiority- for Corso learns Balkan failed to open the gate because one engraving was a forgery- this engraving depicts the demonness he copulates with, riding a dragon (possibly a depiction of the whore of Babylon of Revelation) and pointing towards the opened gate- Corso succeeds where everyone else fails because of a little demonic help from the sacred feminine.

THE OCCULT STUDY

The existence of likely archetypes (either

The Occult Compendium

intentionally or unintentionally placed within the film) is hardly the only allusion to more authentic occult practices within an otherwise standard Hollywood mystery-horror.

The constant allusions to books within the film may be seen as an occult convention indeed- for one thing which occultists have sometimes pointed out, the simple fact that it requires a great deal of study- is also found within this film, where Corso ingests information constantly while other characters do not- perhaps a statement about why they have themselves failed in their quest to comprehend this demonic knowledge. This is possibly reading too much into the film (where Corso is employed by book collectors in the first place) but it is still worth mentioning.

THE STRONG FEMALE (WITCH)

There are, of course, as with any occult related movies of the genre, numerous other conventions related to the occult contained herein, the archetype of the strong female (witch) character is in full swing with "The Girl" (Emmanuele Seigner) and Liana Telfer both sharing such traits.

The Occult Compendium

In the realm of history, of course, a strong female aspect (and the feminine in general) was identified with the occult.

This is one half falsehood (from the burning times) and one half genuine truth: which bears further explanation...

The false half: The notion among the medieval (and post medieval) peoples of the western world that any woman who rebelled, or disobeyed, or was strong (and such things flew in the face of their own interpretation of biblical dogma) was suspected of witchery- that they held orgies in the shadows at night, flew under the full moon by use of various ointments, and so forth.

This falsehood possibly (probably) lies in the medicinally adept women of the time, whose medicinal abilities extended from healing minor wounds or sicknesses, to seemingly defeating death itself, poisoning enemies, causing miscarriages amongst women who did not wish to bear child- that such powers were foreign to the largely illiterate population until well into the 1800s (or later in

The Occult Compendium

some areas) is clear- and that they feared such power is equally clear.

The true half: Within the genuine teachings of the occult the woman is a feared, respected symbol of the occult itself- partially explained to me by Zeena Schreck (a Tantric Buddhist and Setian, leader of the Setian Liberation Movement, among other endeavors) as follows: That the female is able to give birth to the male or female, but the male is not capable of giving birth to either of them.

My take on this extends further- that the generational, creative capacity of the male is limited while for the female, these forces are more or less unlimited- the female creates and destroys, but in an archetypal sense the male may only destroy, unless he is making use of feminine energy, often in the form of an actual female (at least, can only destroy in a spiritual sense.)

THE NINTH GATE: THE NINE MONTHS OF GESTATION

When Dean Corso copulates with his demoness

The Occult Compendium

compatriot, he is unlocking the ninth gate itself- for the Nine may in fact refer to the nine months of pregnancy, with the entire film revolving around sexual symbolism.

Corso is repeatedly frustrated (along with all other protagonists) in his quest to fulfill the occult goal of unlocking the gate- and here we may, if we delve deeper, observe why this is: Simply put, not one of the characters in the film is involved in any sort of sexual relationship, except for Liana Telfer, whose own sexuality has no purpose except to control others, and whose marital state is left in question as in the opening scene her ailing husband hangs himself, referenced as a possible result (by Corso's words) of her husband finding her in bed with her bodyguard.

Once Corso is able to find a more mystical sexual involvement, the gate is already unlocked, for his sexual act was not merely the result of carnal lust, or want of power or money, as all other characters are obsessed with, but the result of a deeper understanding- that his liberation and enlightenment itself hinged upon such acts.

The Occult Compendium

THE ORDER OF THE SILVER SERPENT

The Order of the Silver Serpent itself may be seen as a reference to the more genuine occult- although a brief explanation only is sufficient of this more minor detail.

The serpent may be found first, as the tempter of Eden, inviting liberation and knowledge, for Polanski's film treats other characters, not the occult itself, as harmful and negative- in itself lending itself to a more pseudo-Sumerian view of the less-than-evil nature of Satan or demonic forces.

We may also see a serpentine reference in the medically significant, Greek pagan derived, rod of Asclepius- the serpent twining around the rod and representing healing (which regarding the pagan symbol was seen as only partly herbal/surgical, while the other, more important aspect was seen as coming from the gods, or similar mystic conduits for healing power.)

Of course serpent imagery is hardly limited to these examples, but there are far too many for a short work.

The Occult Compendium

CORSO IS SAMAEL, "THE GIRL" IS LILITH

Dean Corso himself might be taken to represent the spiritual embodiment of Samael- the male counterpart of Lilith, represented by "The Girl" and just as much a mystery throughout the film as Lilith is to theology unless a person also examines Sumerian mythology and the Zohar as well.

The ultimate coming together of these polar forces- Corso as Samael (or perhaps the Devil) and The Girl as Lilith (or perhaps some other vessel, maybe even a tip of the hat to *Rosemary's Baby* where the woman impregnated by Satan is just a regular human being) results in a potent admixture of mystic forces, cracking open the gate guarding enlightenment itself.

It is not quite clear what the opening of the gate represents- taken sexually it regards birth (perhaps Corso's rebirth and understanding that his life has been led in error) while taken at a more literal level, it may represent the opening of the gates of Hell, either to herald the birth of the antichrist, or to admit Corso to a quick afterlife spent in company with Satan.

The Occult Compendium

SUMMATION

To ignore the occult content within *Ninth Gate* would be folly- even the most jaded viewer will at least understand that the film itself is, literally, about a book written by Lucifer and used to conjure him.

The symbolism and archetypes used, however, fit in so well with an occult philosophy, that one has to wonder if all of this appears by drastic coincidence or whether there was a reasoning or planning that went into it- and if so for what purpose?

We cannot be quite sure, perhaps Polanski inserted it for his own amusement, or perhaps he himself practices some sort of magick and felt it would be good to represent it in the film- perhaps he is oblivious and this material was all subconsciously submitted to film form at the behest of some other sort of entity he was not aware of.

CHAPTER V

Sumerian Creation

TIMELINE

Sumeria established: 4000-2900BC
Eridu Genesis written: 2150BC
Organized Judaism forms: 2000BC
Epic of Gilgamesh written: 1800sBC
Jewish Pentateuch with Genesis written: 500BC
Jesus supposedly dies: 33-35AD
Earliest possible speculated date for the biblical gospels: 60CE (Gospel of Mark)
Earliest known date for gospel fragment: 125CE (Gospel of John)

The Occult Compendium

This text is a guide to the original knowledge of the first mesopotamian empire, replete with its cultural overtones found to this very day in the form of judaism, christianity, and islam- perverting and inverting this original, progenitor form to the point of uselessness with fear and guilt, to control the population. This text recognizes that, either, this population control is cosmic, and derives from our original creation from hominids by extra terrestrial life forms, or that it is archetypal, and that early spiritual knowledge over time was manipulated by man, to control other men.

THE TRUE REVELATION

It is true that the race known as homo sapiens is indeed an enslaved entity- religion, culture, government, seek to undermine the truly individualistic, to grind down the unique, and to relegate mankind to a breed of cattle to continue its slavelike existence in the absence of the same extra terrestrial forces that engineered it in the first place.

Modern man has great admiration for the empires of

The Occult Compendium

antiquity, one can hardly pass through a history course without multiple mentions of the Romans, the Macedonians, Greece, Persia, Egypt, and others- but there is one empire which existed long ago which receives little mention, possibly because of the connotations of their teachings, which any sufficiently advanced child should be able to see.

The Sumerian inscriptions and stories which archaeology has amassed tells a very strange story of mankind- we see some parallels in these stories to Aboriginal cultures in Australia and even among the Native Americans- tales of beings from (literally) the sky, of semihumanoid appearance, which bred through sex in a way similar to humans, and we see multiple parallels between these stories and other religions which seem to have- either deliberately or inadvertently- perverted and reversed the meaning of such tales, while keeping essentially the same content wholly intact.

Before discounting this as myth (which it may very well be) one must consider however the Sumerian creation stories, as well as various figures and words from several languages and how they related to derive the true

The Occult Compendium

importance of Sumerian religion as it relates to christianity, islam, and judaism- indeed the text you hold in your hands would be, if properly propagated to the masses, the most revolutionary religious text since the bible itself was compiled at the council of Nicea.

THE CREATION STORY OF SUMERIA

The Sumerians believed mankind was created, essentially, as a slave race to mine resources for a race of godlike individuals they call the annunaki- their tales range from having sex with, and/or being engineered by these individuals, to themselves witnessing the existence of what the Sumerians termed "ape people," to a tale roughly commensurate with the great flood, to others dealing with a doppelganger of the story of Eden.

These slavelike early humans were apparently mistreated by the gods above- for the gods had created mankind so as to avert the necessity of themselves laboring for resources- one can perhaps, if the Sumerian tales hold even a modest kernel of truth, assume that the early megalithic structures we see at the dawn of civilization, were

The Occult Compendium

the result not of human kings and their slaves, but rather hordes of homo sapiens endowed with alien technology, laboring away to construct structures which had some sort of cosmic use to the races above.

Their mentions of ape people are eerily similar to the notion of remnant neanderthals- indeed, if one takes these stories at face value, you'd conclude that neanderthals did not die out but were deliberately bred out of existence to create demigod individuals capable of understanding that went beyond making simple stone tools, spears, and structures of thatch and animal skins.

The fact that so many early cultures seem to, without any communication between them, have created megaliths, agriculture, and spirituality, has always been a daunting challenge for science to explain- what motivated the natives of Brazil, Egypt, Mesopotamia, and other regions, to build mounds, pyramids, and other megaliths? What possible purpose do they serve, when some of them do not serve an astrological importance, but are merely dome shaped mounds or pyramids without, seemingly, any use? Why did so many civilizations develop agriculture and selective breeding capabilities, thousands of miles removed from one

The Occult Compendium

another, without encountering any other cultures which had already done so?

The belief that proto-human hominids evolved out of Africa millions of years ago is all but proven, there is little debate that homo erectus and other species evolved here and moved elsewhere- but thus far, anthropology has yet to develop a comprehensive theory that explains how, over the course of a fairly short period of time, mankind evolved such intelligence- did one aberrant mutant with increased neural folding merely spontaneously evolve, outcompete all the other primitive stone-tool wielding apes, and replicate into oblivion?

The eerie coincidences we see with human creation in Sumerian lore, and other groups, is uncanny; even more of importance, is one fact that few if any christians realize is completely factual, but which they ought to have noticed by now:

"And God said, Let us make man in OUR image, after OUR likeness: and let them have dominion over the fish of the sea, and over the fowl of the air, and over the cattle, and over all the earth, and over every creeping thing

The Occult Compendium

that creepeth upon the earth."

Supposedly, christianity is a monotheistic religion with a singular creator figure as their god- why then do we see here this plural reference?

In reality, in the original Hebrew bible, which has been mistranslated into oblivion by hundreds of languages, and self righteous political entities, the word used in this passage is ELOHIM, which is best understood as a plural noun, indicating here that god is not one individual, singular entity, and that this plural reference is neither a mistake nor a mistranslation, but that literally, there are... MULTIPLE GODS.

The Sumerians, who before a word of the bible was penned, had already told essentially the same creation story and stories about Eden and the flood, have a simple explanation- there isn't one god, there are multiple god-LIKE figures, literally from outer space, or the sky, which created mankind.

The Occult Compendium

THE GARDEN OF EDEN IS A SUMERIAN STORY

The story of the garden of Eden is well known within christianity- the serpent tempts Adam and Eve, they fall out of grace, and are cursed, but we see some eerie similarities between Sumeria and Judaism in the following.

The Sumerians refer to the first man as Adamu, the Jews refer to him as Adam.

The Sumerians envisioned such a location as near multiple rivers, and bearing a plant which imparted knowledge, so do the Jews centuries later.

The Sumerians tell, in the Epic of Gilgamesh, that the land is full of precious jewels, just as the bible suggests.

The Sumerians in The Myth of Enki and Ninhursag describe the area as a garden, just as the bible does with Eden.

The Sumerian usage is at least tenuously identified with the cedars of Lebanon- the book of Ezekiel also seems

The Occult Compendium

to indicate Lebanon as an Eden location.

So we can see these similarities– between Sumerian tales and Judaist tales (the former coming into existence at least many centuries before Judaism penned so much as a word) are, if coincidental, the most spectacular example of coincidence in existence– were two texts to be submitted in any decent university, by two different students, bearing the same level of similarity, both students would be indicated as having copied off of one another– but the christians refuse to see this, partly out of principle, and partly because of the general ignorance of Sumeria in the general population. We see, for example, with the obvious disinformation campaign of Zeitgeist, that any claims that pagan groups influenced so much as a word of the bible, will be compared to the more obviously flawed similarities of modern day conspiracy theorists– in such powerful ways that to make a very SOUND comparison between Genesis and Sumerian mythology, is seen as the same level of "tinfoil hat wearing nonsense" by both religious folks, and skeptics of religion.

The Occult Compendium

SATAN IS GOD, GOD IS SATAN

The Sumerian tales also seem to indicate the familiar Satan/serpent figure of Eden was actually the benevolent, rebellious figure of Ea, a cosmic rebel roughly identified with certain other pagan figures including both the perverted figure of Satan, and the unperverted sanskrit SATYA. This figure encouraged Adamu and his female counterpart to eat of the forbidden plant- for Ea knew that the garden of Eden was not actually a paradise, but a sort of prison- with the blackmail of early human life being that as long as they obeyed their masters, and slaved away at the land, their physical needs would be taken care of- that they would have an unlimited food supply which they did not have to toil to obtain- they were as children, and did not need to think, because their creators, although they treated their creation like cattle, did not let them starve.

Ea, a rebellious deity, had formed what was called the brotherhood of the serpent (another extrabiblical serpent reference!) their goal was the liberation of mankind- Adamu ate the fruit, gained the knowledge that he was a slave, and that he had the ability to better his position, and the vengeful

The Occult Compendium

creators abandoned ship after "cursing" Adamu and forcing him to till the earth to obtain foodstuffs.

The Sumerian tales essentially state this: That the figure of Satan in Ea is actually a benevolent, divine, and helpful being, and the savior of all mankind, and that the creature(s) worshiped by modern religions are actually rapacious, evil, enslaving beings which want mankind to serve them in the physical realm.

We will also see- the very word SATAN in the modern sense is fairly perverted itself- for it seems to have entered the lexicon of western usage on the back of the sanskrit term SATYA which actually means enlightened, as in Satya Yuga, the golden, enlightened age of the Hindu calendar, with the opposite, Kali Yuga, being the current age of spiritual darkness and materialism. SATAN also appears to coincide with at least one other cosmic rebel in antiquity- the Egyptian figure of Seth, a lord of the night still venerated by some mystic traditions in a literal, theistic or semi-theistic sense.

The Occult Compendium

SATAN OR EA IS A POSITIVE FORCE

One challenge a person can make to a religious christian concerning Satan is to ask them where in the bible specifically Satan does anything evil.

They may mention the story of Eden, but Genesis is fairly clear that the entity of the garden is not anthromorphic but appears literally as a physical serpent (easily explained if you assume this tale is based on Sumerian mythology/legend.) They may mention Revelation, but any serious theological scholar has already learned that the book of Revelation is so spurious in sourcing and claims, that it was nearly rejected at the Council of Nicea, and continues to be debated to this day in terms of validity- with large and growing numbers of theists claiming the entire thing is either fabricated or symbolic.

They may also mention a certain passage about Lucifer falling from heaven. (Luke 10:18)

This is problematic when you realize that in the original translation to Latin, Lucifer is actually being used to

The Occult Compendium

describe Jesus in this passage, and is also used to describe a dead Babylonian king (Isaiah 14:12) The term itself is not a noun but an adjective, and merely means "light bearer" (also found as the Greek "Phosphoros.") This was mistranslated centuries ago.

In fact, the bible never depicts Satan as overly malevolent except in the book of Job, where he is acting under the command of god himself, and acts in this manner only to tempt a man who will be later rewarded. In reality, through a serious study of the bible, we see the creator god (or multiple deities as we have already explained) as malevolent, frequently causing disasters, wars, and plagues or famines to devastate populations which subsequently go extinct or suffer untold misery.

In reality, the "good guy" of the bible is the same tempter who liberated mankind in the first place- the Sumerian Ea in the form of a serpent, just as Sumerian myth told centuries before Genesis existed, while the perverted Elohim/Jehovah figure(s) are unimaginably malevolent.

The Occult Compendium

HELL DOES NOT EXIST

The term "Hell" is perhaps the most confused of all- it has for millennia been used to scare the laypeople into compliance with the seemingly deliberately perverted gospel of lies laid down by modern jews, muslims, and christians, as well as countless sects and cults which break off of any of those three, but still use the same outdated, backwards moral systems.

We can identify Hell as a place of fire, burning, torment, where the wicked go when they are deceased, which is eternal, and which is overseen and arbitrated by spirits of darkness.

However Hell is taken from four different terms, from three different cultures!

The word itself comes from the Norse HEL, which merely means grave, or place of rest (after death.)

The idea of Hell as eternal comes from the Hebrew SHEOL, which is roughly the same as Hel, merely a place

The Occult Compendium

folks go when they die, to be purged of sin before entering paradise.

The fire aspect comes from the Hebrew GEHENNA which was a real physical location outside of Jerusalem where trash was burned; this was used as a metaphor (IE: The souls of the wicked are no better than to be burned to ash in Gehenna) but somewhere along the line this was mistranslated literally.

The idea of darkness, torment, and plural demigod-like entities of a nonhuman nature comes from the Greek Tartaros, of a similar nature- a Hellenic location well known to the Romans who conquered and adapted Greek religion, and to the Jews living under Roman authority at the supposed time of Jesus.

The origins of Hell are clear, but twofold in possibility: Either the idea was created by mankind to enslave his fellow man with fear and reinforce culture, or it was developed by some other force (suggested by the Sumerians as the Annunaki) for identical reasons, to enforce a culture of slavery. The gnostic gospel of Nicodemus explains that Hell is neither eternal nor a place of suffering, and is probably closer to truth (if such a location even exists) than any canonized text or religious sermon.

THE REAL JESUS AS A COSMIC REBEL LIKE THE SUMERIAN EA WAS

Whether an actual Jesus existed is a matter of great theological and historical debate- the most likely scenario sees a sort of revolutionary cult or social reform leader in Judaea around the same time who later got deified by overly zealous followers, or else was used politically by Rome to satisfy the rebelling Jews, whose own philosophical texts taught that the Jews would eventually have a savior to lead them out of captivity under Rome, after which they would become a dominant power. It seems likely that at least half of the new testament tales of Jesus were borrowed from other solar messianic figures, which were then overlapped onto texts which had already been in used by genuinely Jesus-following groups, making a hermetic teacher and social reformer into the son of Jehovah.

The same christian groups who applaud Jesus and seek in any way possible to emulate his characteristics have

The Occult Compendium

become a jumbled mess of political, social, and arbitrary religious ritual and mumbo jumbo- we see no clearer distinction between the seminomadic, seemingly hermetic Jesus Christ, and the ways of the modern churches, than the bulletproof popemobile, or the gold-gilded crosses used by catholic services, or by the bigoted, hateful rhetoric of the protestant clergy in their megachurches, or in the fine jewelry and raiments of the orthodoxy- indeed there seem to be few if any real "christians" if we define a christian as "one who emulates the teachings of Jesus as laid down in the bible."

The real face of Jesus, if we, like so many christians, take the bible at face value, is actually one of a rebellious individual who spurned all religious authority, practiced a form of primitive communism, had absolutely no respect for, or admiration for, conventional moral laws or dogma, and who spent a great deal of time wandering the streets or steppe with prostitutes, bums, and laborers who would likely have been illiterate- a Jesus which likely reeked of body odor, wore cheap, ratty garments, and was frequently hungry- very different from the white skinned, perfect, halo-bearing and healthy Jesus of all church statues and depictions, a Jesus which appears as Germanic or Anglo

The Occult Compendium

Saxon as any Nazi youth.

In reality, the teachings of Jesus roughly mimic the Sumerian Ea- a rebel which deliberately opposed authority, even going so far as to sardonically mock them upon numerous occasions, who had more respect for a drunken leper or unrepentant prostitute than for a Pharisee, Roman official, or authority figure.

This reality of Jesus has been all but lost in the modern age, where every priest and pastor is expected to be spotless, blemishless, and just the outward pinnacle of everything "Christlike." Indeed, much of this nonsense is just the result of Pan-European cultural ideals masquerading as spirituality.

The church would be sorely displeased if folks worshiped or followed the teachings of the authentic Jesus Christ- for this figure would abolish physical churches, public prayers, and political activism- the church would no longer be able to grub after money and would be rendered powerless in the face of secular authority which Jesus surely would not have considered any concern of the church in the first place as evidenced by his teachings.

The Occult Compendium

In fact, it seems unlikely Jesus would even approve of the existence of christianity if you take the new testament as his actual teachings- even less if we use apocryphal, gnostic texts which depict a very humanistic Jesus who essentially taught the same laws that modern Satanists or Thelemites teach this very day- boiled down to "Don't hurt or impose on anyone and you can do whatever you want."

Intelligently speaking, to follow the teachings of Jesus, rather than to worship or venerate his corpse, is the means, and societal and tribal peace, rather than obtaining eternal favor with god, is the goal.

IN VENERATION OF ARCHETYPAL REBELLION

From three perspectives, we can see the benefit of social, individual, and tribal rebellion.

From the perspective of the Sumerians, the first cosmic act of rebellion led to the first act of human rebellion, the end result being the liberation of mankind; thus, the development of society, technology, and individualism was

The Occult Compendium

possible- all modern sciences, technologies, and other innovations are the direct result of a figure which can roughly be equated to Satan.

From the perspective of the genuine early christian movement (not the modern, political, perverted perspective) Jesus himself was a rebel of unimaginable levels, spurning religious authority, politics, wealth, and all forms of moral dogma- through this rebellion he founded a short lived but semi-utopian movement whose members were later, unfortunately, usurped by the Romans in the form of Catholicism, which subsequently fractured and has led to thousands of equally invalid transmogrifications and perversions of the original, human, mortal Jesus and his own form of individualistic anarcho communism.

From a purely humanistic perspective, rebellion itself is merely a practice in progress, which follows the same basic principles as genetic evolution, with successive improvements on technology or philosophy being reserved according to how well they work, unless they are deliberately suppressed and perverted, as we see the Romans did with genuine christianity, and as all extant abrahamic movements have attempted to do with the original Sumerian stock which they evolved from.

Some modern movements have attempted to replicate this cosmic rebellion- notably the Church of Satan, which unfortunately was sabotaged by misunderstanding and greed, leading to the entire administrative organization itself to become little more than a money scheme involving minor celebrities and occasional press coverage. The originally good idea eventually reeked with materialism, partly as a result of pressure from evangelical movements in the 1980s which forced it to become reactionary to their perturbations.

CONCLUSION

Regardless of whether one puts stock in Sumerian legend, or biblical mythology, and regardless of whether one venerates any sort of messianic or deified figures in their life, several conclusions can be made regarding Sumeria, the Annunaki, the bible, Jesus, and society itself.

The Sumerian creation stories are the basis for the material from which Genesis was made.

The Occult Compendium

The Jews, after migrating west from the Sumerian region, retained much of this creation story, but reversed its meaning: either due to cultural stimuli, or, if theism is correct and the original stories true, because of influence by evil or nefarious cosmic forces.

The historical Jesus roughly equates to the Sumerian Ea, and Ea roughly equates to Satan if one strips Satan of negative connotations.

Rebellion (or nonconvention) is the force behind cultural evolution just as aberrant mutants drive biological evolution- and this symbol is identified in some of the earliest religious texts as a positive force, and the reason mankind exists as it does to this day.

The modern mainstream abrahamic religious groups (judaism, islam, and christianity) pervert the meaning of languages and cultures to their own original cultural ends.

Mistranslations have resulted in a confusing slew of terms associated with Hell, Satan, and other figures (such as Demon, which comes from the Greek "Daemon" which

The Occult Compendium

more closely means ghost.)

Because of all of this and more, and because large portions of the bible are probably taken from Sumeria (not to mention dozens of other cultures as scholars can freely study, especially from Zoroastrianism and Roman political cults) the bible cannot be considered a literalistic historical guide in large part, and, if theism rather than atheism is true, we were likely created, as the Sumerians and other early groups believed, by extra terrestrial life of some form, which was malevolent, and we roughly mirror this cosmic race, being composed mainly of conformists with a few rebellious individuals who drive all progress.

The irony of this text is that, although most of these conclusions are based on logical observation, or even established fact, they will be reviled and even scoffed at by modern judeochristian or islamic groups that stand to benefit the most from this same form of cosmic liberation, for the simple reason that the abrahamic religious communities have been so indoctrinated by politically dogmatic, greedmongering priests, preachers, and pastors, that they have come to view fairly obvious truth as lies from the same Satan that they don't even know the origins of.

The Occult Compendium

For while it is obvious within archaeology that Sumerian religion predates Judaism by at least 1,000 and probably over 3,000 years, and while the similarities in this predating system with judaism are more than coincidental and will be recognized as such by rational individuals, the religious groups most affected by such a revelation are unlikely to overcome the fear of perdition which permeates their entire religious movement, to the point where it has become a moral infraction to even question the religious authorities in question, or the validity or sourcing of biblical accounts. The muslims and christians which worship progressively more off-track deities and are increasingly confused over linguistic and cultural terms than the jews themselves when they borrowed Sumerian lore, have become so zealous they will likely never even bother to study Sumeria.

Note: while much of this information is pointed to by conspiracy theorists, and new age groups, as evidence of a reptilian or masonic cult movement designed to cause humans to worship Satan, I do not personally offer this as an explanation although I do admit it is likely such truths about the origins of abrahamic cults are deliberately hidden and

The Occult Compendium

disinformation about them spread to the population (as with Zeitgeist, which was too fatally flawed to have been created by serious study and was almost certainly deliberately mixed with 9-11 conspiracy theories to derail continued speculation about Mithra or Horus) in order to prevent them from propagating this original, rebellion-driven spiritual path which would doom all organized religion and would prevent the systematic greed-driven corruption of the social and political structure by folks who usurp power through religious allusion in the first place.

CHAPTER VI

The Psychic Arts

ASTRAL PROJECTION

The process of astral projection has been confusing to many people in the western world for generations- often spoken of but rarely properly explained, while the eastern Tantrics and Hindus take the ability for granted, often including it in their more hidden, mystic teachings, the kind most western practitioners are only exposed to after grueling levels of meditative practice.

In reality, the process is fairly simplistic, with several ways to actually access this astral realm. Some groups even speak of a sort of archived memory within this realm, which contains all egregores and thoughts created by intelligent beings, with access to this spiritual world limited to ones own abilities of self control. Although this astral archive is rumored to exist, the west has not yet seemingly found a reliable tantric or hesychasist source to verify its ancient roots, so it may be new age hokum.

The Occult Compendium

However, it is no secret that some individuals possess the ability to travel outside of their body- either into an astral form, or through the remote viewing process, in which they travel only along the physical plane. There are several variants on how to access an astral state, three of which will be discussed here.

SLEEP DEPRIVATION

Although it is not medically recommended, sleep deprivation seems to be one of the more simple methods used, including within certain tantric circles, to provoke an astral experience: the individual typically uses a combination of fasting and meditation to achieve this state, in which, either through hallucination or psychic event, they are spiritually removed from their body, and enter a vivid "waking dream" state.

Lucid dreaming often acts as a sort of precursor to astral travel: some individuals claim they can do both on a fairly regular basis, and they do seem to coincide with one another, but for those who do not normally have lucid dreams, depriving oneself from sleep for an extended period

The Occult Compendium

of time (about two days) can cause lucid dreams, and thereafter, powerful visions or astral travel, initiated or involuntary.

This process should only be used, however, under the guidance and watchful eye of a trained physician, as it could also lead to medical problems of a particularly dire nature.

PSYCHEDELICS

Because psychedelic substances were outlawed by corrupt politicians in the western world, many individuals have traveled to eastern locations to partake in spiritual rituals in which astral projection may play a role- among the central African shaman, astral travel under the guidance of a shaman while invoking their deity, Bwiti, is fairly common, using a psychotropic known as *Iboga* . The Siberian tribes partake in *Amanita Muscaria* to provoke similar results, while the ancient Hindus and Buddhists surely would have been well acquainted with numerous substances native to their region, which may explain the routinely psychedelic art they use to represent their deities.

The Occult Compendium

In the happy land on the West side of the pond, in the United States, the consumption of both substances is illegal, but the acquisition and sale is, amusingly, not considered so- I have myself left my body during makeshift rituals using amanita mushrooms, envisioning vast expanses of black, empty space, permeated by gridlike lines, crystalline objects, and other strange figures. Deliriants like *Datura Stramonium* also create a strange state which may induce such visions, although it significant toxicity makes it useless for most individuals. *Salvia Divinorum* was very popular in the west until it was recently banned, for the same astral purposes, in which reality essentially caves in on itself.

Of course, the most potent of all would be DMT, a substance derived from *psychotria viridis* or other tropical plants, and usually mixed with other plant species to potentiate its effects- users often describe a sort of psychedelic dreamworld akin to the tales told by those who have practiced astral projection, with strange astral beings attending to them, including a "species" referred to by psychonauts as "Machine Elves" which encourage the individual to create existence through pure willpower, or through spoken words. Those who have remained skeptical

The Occult Compendium

and dismissed such reports often overlook the fact that such beings are encountered frequently by users of DMT, even if they have not previously heard of this phenomenon.

MEDITATION

Of course, the most authentically eastern methods of astral travel involve months or years of training in meditation- which may be combined with other spiritual elements within their practices. Western audiences, obsessed with technology, a "quick fix" to their problems, and snap decisions, find the process of merely relaxing and emptying ones mind to be problematic and difficult, often beginning such a task only to quit on their first try.

The positions most commonly used by eastern individuals while in meditation vary, but are normally some variation of the following:

The individual sits in lotus pose, or with their legs crossed, indian style.

The arms are kept loose, and slightly away from the

The Occult Compendium

body, while the hands relax in the lap, usually facing upwards, with the thumbs crossing.

The tongue must be rested against the upper palate behind the teeth.

The head is slightly downwards, with the crown of the skull facing directly upwards.

In all variations, the individual then focuses upon a sound, upon an object, or upon "nothingness." In my own experience, I have found most meditation to be difficult at best, but one method prescribed to me that worked fairly well, was to focus upon a candle flame: the slight movements of the flame help to induce a trancelike state, in which the mind empties itself. (This should not be confused with hypnosis/mesmerism: It seems unlikely a person would accidentally put themselves into a hypnotic trance while meditating.)

For astral travel to occur, the mind must at once focus intently, and unfocus, in a manner similar to "willing" oneself to such a state without consciously doing so- a confusing characteristic which serves as a severe

The Occult Compendium

stumblingblock to those who wish to practice this eastern artform.

For those who have studied Tai Chi or similar bodily training, they may note that the poses used for meditation echo those in such forms, except that you are sitting down rather than moving about- indeed, having practiced Tai Chi, it's fairly easy to see how the two are related.

One method which has been described to travel in the astral plane involves relatively simple methods: The same position is used as for meditation, but the focus point should be upon the body itself- the individual must follow a very simple routine:

-They feel the weight of the air (or gravity) around them.

-They then feel the sensation of their skin, consciously.

-Once this sensation has been focused upon for a period of time, they must then feel "beyond" the sensation, almost as if they were feeling the air around them.

The Occult Compendium

–After a short period of time, if they are deep enough in a trance state, they will actually leave their body, and will perceive themselves as having awoken, only to then see their own body still in meditation– at this point they normally are afraid or lose focus, and snap out of it in exactly the same manner as they would a lucid dream.

There is another method– in which the individual begins to meditate while lying flat on their back, arms at their sides. This sleep position often causes lucid, waking dreams, but the goal of the individual should be to attempt this until they no longer snap awake when it happens, but instead are then free to use their mind to explore a vivid dream world.

Those versed in psychology may recognize that these methods rely on a state of temporary hypnogogia, in which the person is transitioning from being asleep to being awake– a state also used by hypnotists, in which the subconscious and conscious are both most easily accessed. Some skeptics have claimed that astral travel is essentially a hallucination or vivid dream in which the subconscious is accessed directly by the conscious mind– whether this is true or not has yet to be

The Occult Compendium

explained, but the method does indeed work.

THE SERPENT FIRE

The essence of the eastern spirituality itself relies heavily on sex- with the pre-colonial tantrics, in some circles, often using orgies and copious levels of alcohol or drugs to achieve spiritual power. While these groups are now mostly underground or limited to pseudospiritual cults, we have enough of their material to emancipate, for a western audience, one of the most interesting of all features of their spirituality.

"The Serpent Fire" refers to the kundalini, an energy awakening of insane power, which is often glossed over by western practitioners of eastern spiritual practices, possibly because it is "too intense" or possibly because the eastern teachers of such western individuals do not wish for them to have access to these more arcane teachings (or they assumed western audiences would laugh at the concept, and thus chose not to include it.)

To awake the serpent fire is said to be dangerous- a

The Occult Compendium

process which can lead to insanity, as during the process an individual may become distracted by visions and, due to the process being incomplete, essentially fry their brains or cause other bodily harm to themselves- I cannot personally account for this as fact or fiction, but testing it could, if such tales are true, in essence end my ability to report them.

Through meditation and other things designed to increase the pranic life force of mind and body, and often through a vegetarian or vegan, organic diet (to cleanse and purify the pineal gland- which will be discussed more shortly) the body readies itself to achieve kundalini awakening- to accept and transmit the serpent fire.

The pineal gland is seen as the primary transmitter and receiver of such energies- and the importance of this gland differs between several groups:

The Hindu or Buddhist movements see it more as a spiritual vessel, and believe that the mind must be spiritually purified in order to properly use this gland to connect with higher planes, as during the process of kundalini awakening, the chakras are hyperactivated.

The Occult Compendium

The new age movements, who also practice astral travel in various ways, see it more biologically, indicating that an inorganic, non-vegetarian diet causes the gland to calcify- and this is based upon reality, as large numbers of people, through their diet or activities, do indeed suffer from this condition, causing the gland to become less fully functioning.

Certain other groups believe the pineal gland releases DMT, a substance I have already discussed as a potent psychedelic, and aid in astral travel and lucid dreaming. If these individuals are correct in this belief, it is no small surprise that the pineal gland is important in all psychic arts.

A long process is involved with awakening kundalini, but the essence, at its root, relies upon the purification of the pineal gland, the opening of the spinal column through an energy chain called the sushumna nadi, and the use of various yoga and meditation exercises.

The end result of this long process is said to be connection to the divine, as well as the reception of various psychic skills, including the ability to travel along the astral

The Occult Compendium

plane- there are numerous eastern teachers who claim to teach this skill, although the difficulty lies, as always, in determining if any of these individuals are dedicated to true enlightenment practices, or if they are primarily motivated by a desire to make a profit off of gullible, spiritually disconnected westerners.

The main goal, however, of all yogic processes is not normally the reception of psychic abilities, but rather inner peace and enlightenment, which do not necessarily require the ability to travel along the astral plane- a singular skill which may more readily be attained through much more simplistic efforts, which would appeal to a western audience.

Various sexual rituals are identified with the Serpent Fire- and the kundalini is said to manifest as sexual drive- for which sexual magick itself is fairly useful, and a great many texts have been made on the subject, with varying degrees of reliability- but most revolve around the use of willpower during a sexual ritual, to, in effect, open the channels to such energies.

Occultists may notice a great number of rituals revolve around the offering of sexual fluids or sexual lust to

The Occult Compendium

various deities and idols- a process which in many cases is an adaptation of the kundalini/ serpent fire process.

TELEKINESIS

Telekinesis- or the ability to move objects with ones mind- is often seen as the crown jewel of the psychic arts- with folks claiming such powers even in ancient times, and a renewed interest in the cold war, along with interest in remote viewing.

There are various methods which have been prescribed to make use of this power- some of which are described hereafter. It should be noted that in some circles, levitation is seen as a natural progression of telekinesis- literally the ability to achieve telekinesis not on external objects, but upon oneself.

THE TRADITIONAL METHOD

As with astral projection, the most common method of attempting telekinesis is roughly similar to other psychic

The Occult Compendium

methods, making use of focus and willpower. Typically it follows several discrete steps:

An individual will focus upon an object to be moved (smaller objects are seen as easier to perform this skill on than larger ones) meditating upon it visually.

They will then "force" their willpower into it, by again going into a semi-hypnagogic trancelike state, usually imagining the object beginning to float in accordance with either their imagination, or a gestured movement.

Similarly, the individual sometimes chooses to imagine a light emanating from their body (or from a hand outstretched towards the object) usually of a white or red color, which envelops the object and increases their focus- interestingly, while this seems to be a western convention, it has some roots in the eastern mystic paths, with the idea that pranic energy is sent and received through the palms of ones hands.

The Occult Compendium

MEDITATION AS A TELEKINETIC METHOD

Telekinesis is also achieved by some individuals using a deep meditative state- instead of consciously focusing upon an object, they choose to attempt to move the object by using the same method as described for astral travel.

-The individual relaxes in a meditation posture, stretching their mind out in an attempt to break the connection between self and nonself.

-Once the boundary between the self and the external is weak or nonexistent, the individual attempts to then make a *new* connection with the object itself which is to be moved about. This is claimed to be possible, but only under a very potent state of near-nirvana.

Key to this method is the notion that there is no actual boundary between ones body and mind, and objects within the outside world- a belief common to eastern as well as new-age western sources: This simplifies the process greatly, by assuming that there is no specific physical reason why physical force itself is necessary to affect the mass of an

The Occult Compendium

object or its momentum.

Indeed, when we observe the properties of energy, it's self explanatory that it is not necessary to actually touch an object with another object of mass in order to get it to change its location.

A MOST EASY METHOD

The most simple method that has been described is as follows: To those who already are versed in meditation, the meditation method is most likely more effective for this process, but this one is probably easier for those who do not have the ability to meditate.

The individual should sit in a relaxing position.

A small object should be used– typically a spoon or other quite small metallic object (the metallic characteristic is said to simplify the process.)

Focus upon the object intently, with the eyes half closed, focusing at the same time upon the sound of your

The Occult Compendium

breath.

The hands lay facing upwards in front of the object.

Rather than as described before, imagining a light emanating from the body to the object, imagine a light emanating from the object *to* the body, and entering at the hands. This is far easier because the source of light is in your visual range rather than, say, inside your chest or forehead.

Imagine the light slowly begin to ebb up the arms to the chest- you should not do this consciously, but rather "feel" the light as it enters the arms and chest region- this may manifest as tingling, warmth, or a heavyness.

The light fills the chest, now imagine it reaching the head.

At this point you may get the tactile sensation of touching the object itself- if you have this sensation you are succeeding- if not it may take many tries to get the method to work. Once you feel the object through the empty space between it and your hands, gently, consciously, using willpower alone, guide it in movement.

The Occult Compendium

BEWARE OF FRAUDS

As with any occult or mystic system there are many frauds circulating in print, online, and in the media, who claim extraordinary powers yet have accomplished absolutely nothing in their own spiritual path (if you can even consider them spiritual to begin with.) The occult has its own share of fake gurus, just as the Abrahamic paths have their megachurch pastors or rabid imams.

I have seen people fashion spoons or forks out of gallium (which looks exactly like a steel spoon or fork but melts at just above room temperature) magically "melting" the object by applying friction with their fingers, and convincing crowds they possessed awesome telekinetic powers- a parlor trick which is used in modified form by scientists who will fashion such a spoon and place it in someone's hot coffee- and subsequently melt to the bottom of the cup.

Astral travel likely has its own wishful thinkers- because the process to achieve it tends to elude most people unless they give it serious practice. You can dig up hundreds

The Occult Compendium

of websites offering quick methods to perform any and all of these tricks, and you can surely find those who, for a fee, will gladly give you vague and confusing instructions on how to levitate or throw a chair through the air with your mind.

The only genuine teaching in all of their fraud is that the process takes time and practice in order to work- it would be extraordinary if an individual managed to do any of these things on their first try, or without practice- which immediately makes one think of Kreskin or Gellar and their own obvious fraud. If you desire these happy powers, the best idea is to practice these or similar methods repeatedly- for practice makes perfect.

So mote it be.

CHAPTER VII

The New Satanism

THE NEW SATANISM

When the average person hears another say, simply, "I am a Satanist" their mind is filled with visions of devil worshipers gathered around an open fire, or in the graveyard, huddled near the tombs of the dead, sacrificing infants- this throwback to the Satanic Panic has persisted long past its expiration date. Even the more open minded amongst the population have difficulty wrapping their heads around the topic- assuming without merit that the Satanist is in fact worshiping a christianized version of the ancient Hebrew Devil.

In the 1960s, as the Church of Satan was formed by Anton LaVey, a new philosophy was born- why should the people regret their wrongdoings, if such a thing as absolute 'wrong' even existed? Why should man be burdened with moral laws invented by desert migrants who continuously became enslaved because their own backwards views of the

The Occult Compendium

world were inherently inferior to other cultures they encountered? For a small fee, anyone could join Anton in his circus of bohemian happiness, free now to do as they wished and install upon their soul the mantle of "Satanist."

As time went by, however, the Church was wracked with problems- firstly, that some of their own important members either left or became ambivalent towards its very existence, secondly that the Church, once a bastion of bothering the abrahamists, ended up being little more than a self-service station for the egotistically challenged- a book could be written solely on the topic of the problems plaguing this organization and other, similar "churches," if indeed they can be termed so, since most have no physical buildings beyond administrative centers.

In the most modern sense, Satanism has both grown and floundered- a bizarre thing indeed, for even as the number of people who claim the title grows rapidly (something I have myself witnessed firsthand) the number of people open about being Satanic is remaining stagnant due to pressure from christians and muslims in particular- who normally believe the Satanist is worshiping what they call the Devil. It doesn't help that the majority of the population

The Occult Compendium

retains the 1980s style view of Satanism as a largely negative, cult-like group.

The fact that LaVey's Satanism was, is, and always will be atheistic is a fact that the christian seems unable to comprehend- the very use of the term "Satanic" to describe the movement causes all who behold it to believe it revolves around a form of worship. Equally unhelpful has been the spread of conspiracies involving a supposedly Satanic elite controlling the world- a topic which can be debated, but which surely confuses people, for the use of "Satanist" to describe the purported mind-controlling elite confuses LaVey's atheistic Satanism with some sort of elite, Bohemian-Grove style devil worshiping which always seems to involve tales of kidnapping, freemasons, human sacrifice, and on occasion, reptile-human hybrid aliens.

Thus, it is important to reclaim the title from both the Satan-obsessed christian and the Satan-obsessed conspiracy theorist- to describe, once and for all, a sound moral basis for both the term and the philosophy existing- far from merely a joke to bother judeochristians, Satanism is best seen as one part philosophy, one part way of life, and one part healing campaign for the sick in spirit- sickened

The Occult Compendium

because they have often been told for their
they are fallen, sinful, evil, and bound to
suffering in blazing flames.

The first, foremost, and most utterly important aspect of real Satanism is as an ointment to cure the disease of guilt and fear which runs rampant throughout most of western society- everyone is guilty for something; one man is guilty because he had sex before marriage, another is guilty because he stole a loaf of bread, and everyone is told to feel guilty for their race, their religion, and their creed.

This pandemic guilt that is ravaging society is force-fed to us by those with an ax to grind- every politician who wants to pander picks a racial group, gender, creed, and tells them how sorry he or she is for their plight and promises to help them out (usually at the expense of others) while every special interest group wants to shame its opposition using crude psychological warfare tactics. We are told that we are filthy, low creatures without redeeming quality- the church tells its congregation to feel guilty at every turn, so that they can then extract money from them.

We're a people built up upon a mountain of guilt,

The Occult Compendium

...etimes for things we ourselves never did– we're told to feel guilty because our ancestors might have owned slaves, or killed natives, or killed people in war– a societal trend which can be loosely compared to the biblical concept of a child being guilty for the sins of their ancestor– an unhelpful, shaming, damning aspect of the entire western world which we ought to do our best to cast aside.

The decline of the west has coincided with this nonstop assault of guilt– no longer does the western man stand tall with sword in hand, conquering the barbarians, no longer does he even particularly care to preserve his own culture, feeling mostly ambivalent towards it, told since birth that he is not exceptional, his culture is not superior, and his life is not important and has no cosmic meaning, except that he is a sinner and must repent and give money to god. Here we see a cycle, a self preserving spiral of guilt, for when the western man feels guilty, goes to church, and gives money to it, that money ends up in the pockets of political groups who in turn perpetuate war and crime, so that the man feels ever more guilty and fallen– what a nice cycle this is for the people receiving the money in the first place.

The stronger minds say no to this creeping plague of

The Occult Compendium

decadence and ambivalence- and realize that a culture which does not see itself as superior, and a man equally so that sees himself as just a drone amongst other drones, will die out, his genetic line replaced by those that have more egotistical views- for nature itself is an egoist, and favors the strong and intelligent, wiping out the bloodlines of the lesser. Here we see the birth of a realization, that Satanism at its core is an understanding that being egotistical and looking out for oneself and ones' allies first and foremost is defamed as inappropriate and immoral primarily because those that already control the population would lose everything if man began to practice this form of moral philosophy.

In reality, the same type of "sins" which the average person in the west feels guilty for are more prevalent in a society in which he throws away his well-being, in which he tithes to a church that is beholden only to a dead god and not to the rule of logic or common sense. When rationality is lacking, these unofficial governing bodies, which help control the population through lies, spend their time and money largely on their own selfish endeavors.

Behold the hypocrisy of the megachurch, or of the Vatican- they preach to give, yet they take; they preach

The Occult Compendium

charity from their thrones and in front of thirty foot tall gold plated crosses, they preach about the humility and humbleness of their messiah, while screaming on stage in front of thousands of people, dressed in the purest, cleanest robes, mocking their own redeemer by their behavior.

That jesus himself, were he real and were he to return to Earth, would slaughter these folks first and stomp them out of existence, is fairly clear; if you compare the teachings of the biblical figure with what is said and done by the average minister or preacher today, you can see the enormous disconnect between the two. Especially in the cases of prosperity gospel preachers and those that speak in tongues, rolling around on the floor spouting nonsense, it is clear that the bible's message has been largely forsaken by the so-called christians of today- and this is a hypocritical state which extends further than the christians, to the muslims and jews as well, for none of these groups practice what their prophets and rabbis preached.

I have met a few real christians in my life and most were homeless bums- they actually live like their messiah said to live, in poverty and spurning materialism- and while I myself have zero desire to live such a life, and don't

The Occult Compendium

necessarily even respect it, I can at least respect them for not being of the same caliber of judgmental hypocrites that comprises the average church, where the secretly alcoholic priest or minister sits wide eyed, ranting about theological concepts he does not understand, while the laypeople fidget in their pews, waiting for the sermon to end so they can immediately return to sinning.

Here is the next truth about Satanism- Satanism, beyond its core as both a selfish and liberty-loving bohemian philosophy, is a forsaking of hypocrisy- the removal of the societal trappings of being a "good" or "moral" person and the recognition that man IS a sinner, but that sin is fine, and that man IS selfish, but that this selfishness is not just natural, but even, if kept under some state of self control, even desirable and positive. The world is a wretched, hideous place in some cases- and where this is the case, if you seek you shall find, that it was the hypocrisy of society itself that helped it enter such a fallen state- the biblical moral system might be seen as a self fulfilling prophecy, because individuals think they can be idiots and charlatans six days a week, then pray for forgiveness, and go right back to sinning as soon as the church service is over- abrahamists (namely christians but also muslims and jews) have yet to address this

The Occult Compendium

issue properly.

The christians and so forth are to blame, but not completely, because most of the laypeople and at least a large minority of the preachers and priests misunderstand their own theology- if you ask a dozen christians what it means to be saved, you will get a dozen different answers- even within the same sect, and often within the same church body, opinions on what it means to even be a god fearing christian may differ widely. There are thousands of sects within christianity, and dozens of schools of judaism and islam, something people don't seem to understand- how, then, can anyone take any of these groups at face value, when each espouses that its own way is "right" and others are either wrong or "miss the mark?"

The religious folks of the world scarcely understand their own religion; within this work I will tackle the topic of what constitutes the devil, as well as other sticking points where the christian shows he or she doesn't even understand the underlying theology of the religion itself- these topics confuse the christian especially, for the christian has been told from a young age that to even question the narrative of the church is akin to questioning god- a mortal sin at worst

The Occult Compendium

and at the very least a grave infraction.

Here we must identify several of the sins of the average church.

Firstly, that the churches, particularly the large ones with larger congregations (and especially those that are part of larger networks, such as the Roman Catholics) are hypocritical, telling their congregations to live under a moral standard that they themselves do not adhere to- if we observe the catholics, only their monks and nuns live up to the ascetic standards of the bible, with the upper members of their churches living lives of relative luxury.

Secondly, the churches are political pawns, and intermix with representatives and governments across the world, even outside of the west, and will pay lip service to western values while pushing theocracy in the third world, such as in Africa, where both protestants and catholics have spread their tentacles, sitting by and saying nothing as the mentally ill and nonbelievers are attacked and often killed for their "sins."

Thirdly, the churches are complicit in feeding their

The Occult Compendium

congregations lies, either for a purpose, or because the churches themselves aren't aware of the truth- we could extend this further, saying that because different churches teach such radically different ideas, that only a handful at most are teaching the truth of the gospel (if we argue devil's advocate, pun not intended, and assume there is such a thing as a gospel truth) because these teachings are so often contradictory- situations where churches latch on to dubious "scientific" studies and opinion pieces based not on fact but conjecture serve to illustrate this point further, and they pursue these lies for all issues, whether it be homosexuality, abortion, free speech, secular politics, or any other issue.

Fourthly, the laypeople themselves are utter hypocrites, from the soccer mom having an affair, who begs her god for forgiveness on Sunday and then goes for another drunken fling the next afternoon, to the priest ranting about how bad homosexuals are, and then getting a rubdown in a legally dubious massage parlor the next weekend, to the crack smoking dropout who goes each week to the church, tells god this week "I will throw my pipe away forever" and then goes out to score a rock.

Fifth and finally, that the churches even at times push

The Occult Compendium

their own congregation to accept what they themselves term a sinful life- I can find no single better example than during the dawn of the war in Iraq, when the islamic clerics were telling their followers to blow themselves up for allah, while congregations here in the west were given the functionalist argument that it was okay if their sons signed up to go murder people in the desert for political reasons, because warfare was okay with jesus, and to ignore their own books' admonishment not to kill. This was odd, because those same churches, later on, would also pretend god could hear them as they prayed for the economy to improve, after trillions of dollars were wasted in part because the churches themselves had convinced a large segment of the population that the war was god's will- their shortsightedness was hilarious.

And so there comes a time when we are faced with understanding the caliber of people we have to deal with in this world- they are themselves selfish, but they condemn selfishness and hide it behind a thousand rationalizations all rooted in their feel-good church dogma, and they proclaim that it is wrong to harm others while supporting warfare that kills millions, and they praise humbleness and shun materialism when they go to the mall and purchase cheap and worthless trinkets made in China and Thailand by ten

The Occult Compendium

year old indentured servants.

And yet these same individuals take it upon themselves to judge the Satanist, to tell the Satanist that he or she is wrong, malevolent, evil, materialistic and selfish, and what is worse they are so fooled by their own churches and books that they can do it with a straight face and actually believe that the foolishness pouring from their mouths is true. Here we see the true root of all evil, which is hypocrisy, not money, and which is the unhelpful but good feeling lies which keeps these sheep in line, and keeps them bleating the mantras fed to them by their priests and politicians.

To these folks, it is better by far to lie and not get caught than to truly tell the truth- if you could get them to truthfully tell all the sins they feel guilty for they'd be exiled as pure evildoers, but to the honest Satanist, sinning is only at most a subjective moral wrongdoing, surely not something to dwell on and feel guilty for for your entire life only to be punished eternally by the power of some crazed and tyrannical deity. One doesn't even need to be an atheist to understand that the workings of the cosmos proposed by evangelical christians or radical islamists would result in

The Occult Compendium

having to admit that their gods are evil and that mankind is cast adrift on a sea of madness, created if it is true by those same evil beings.

So the Satanist is not proclaiming death- that is the job of the evil gods of the abrahamists and the church which supposedly represents them, those who are able ought to do what they can to liberate all the slaves in these hellholes whenever possible, assuming it is their will to help their fellow man.

Satanism is a selfish philosophy- so, in a way, is libertarianism, but it is not a philosophy that encourages us to harm others by allowing them to remain enslaved; it is the pinnacle of liberty, the ultimate sacrificial casting off of unstable and often unjust legalism and authority, and the embracing of the beauty of the world, both man-made and natural- and a world of Satanism would surely be a world of peace, where individuals can work either alone or together, without constantly grinding others underfoot.

There is but one weakness in the Satanic ideology, one which has held it back from its potential- and this is the tendency for the ego to rule over the logical, whereas in its perfected form, the ego is ruled by logic, and is more noble in form- such that when we say that a person ought to do as they wish with their life and strive for happiness and advancement, we must also tell them that they ought to strive to understand the world around them, study the philosophers, study the visionaries, read many books, apply themselves to some greater cause- for whereas currently the Satanic community is torn apart by individuals using their ambition for mere gain for gain's sake, and for their ego's sake, it can be united when these quite talented individuals apply that ambition to a noble cause.

THE DEATH OF ELITISM

Having read the last chapter, the reader may get the impression that this new Satanism is built around a purely darwinistic concept, IE that some individuals are worthless or must be destroyed, and that Satanism is a club for those with drastically better abilities and intellect than the general population.

Such are the beliefs of a purely deranged mind- for any individual, given the right mental prompting, is capable

The Occult Compendium

of understanding that they matter, that their views are already valid- Satanism was built around a facade of elitism, with its leadership (if you can truly have a Satanic leader) constantly telling the media and every onlooker that it is necessary to be exceptional in some way to become a Satanist- and while the logical selfishness of Satanism certainly requires an exceptional ability to resist indoctrination into the societies of today (those that have been indoctrinated into the feel-good ethos of everyone being identical and homogeneous cannot easily comprehend Satanism's value) the Satanic movements of yesterday have misused and misconstrued the topic to make themselves seem like a special club for particularly skilled individuals, so that individuals with large egos will sign up, in the belief that it enforces and expands their own supposedly superior abilities.

This facade of elitism has mainly served to destroy every Satanic group that employs it- for how can a large number of extremely egotistical individuals, some or all of which always forget the admonishment to think and use logic alongside their ego, work together, or even necessarily tolerate one another, without constantly competing, subverting one another, in an attempt to gain a following, or obtain what they themselves want, often for the simple sake that they take joy in "winning?"

But these individuals do not seem to understand that the core of Satanism- the very concept by which it was able to exist- is logic, reason, common sense, things that are given lip service by most Satanic groups (for example, "religion makes no sense and there is no evidence that any god exists"- a common understanding amongst Satanists) but in practice, they ignore this entirely, and spend their time selling more memberships.

It is here that we begin to piece together a more adequate Satanic philosophy, and one which is capable of both growing and being appreciated by those who may not even particularly care about their own ego- if Satanism wishes to continue existing as a dynamic and potent force, several basic concepts must be understood by its members.

SATANIC ADMONISHMENTS

First and foremost, is as always the simplistic concept of the ego, of selfishness, of "doing what thou wilt" for a life

The Occult Compendium

lived doing only what others tell you to do, is the life of a slave and often not worth living- in this first concept, the Satanist is admonished to do what they wish to do, to seek pleasure and gain, and to, if necessary, compete with others to obtain it, in a darwinistic approach. The Satanist must be sure of themselves, and either possess or seek to possess the skills they need to survive and thrive in a world which is governed first and foremost by this principle, which we will call for this philosophy's sake, the *biological admonishment.*

Secondly, the above being true, and the ego being the center of the Satanic lifestyle, there comes the second admonishment, which is not necessarily innate or natural, but must temper and rule over the first- in this second concept, we apply the concepts of reason and common sense- what good, after all, is being free physically and mentally, if mind and body are not rooted in any real understanding of the world, and what good is being free but ignorant? In the past, far wiser folks than most today, namely the founders of western civilization itself, from ancient Greece to the founding of the United States, indicated that a well educated population, one with an understanding of and appreciation for both the possession and search for knowledge, was a population that was more free- a society

The Occult Compendium

...the darkness of ignorance will either fall
...archy, or, if knowledge is held only by a
...to a sort of oligarchic meritocracy, in which
individuals who would otherwise succeed, thrive, and be
skilled, are denied, artificially, access to the means to do so.

This second admonishment, to seek knowledge, to learn, to rule the physical desire with common sense and to ask what the consequences of each action can or will be, we will call the *humanistic admonishment.*

The third concept the Satanist must apply, having determined that they are a free, sovereign individual, allowed naturally to do whatever they wish, and having determined to act rationally in doing so (both to prevent their own destruction and the destruction of those around them without need) is also important- namely not to harm others without need.

This concept is generally already well understood by Satanists, and is often repeated, but it cannot be repeated often enough, and it can never be given enough exposure to the mass media and the mass population, which generally do not understand or choose not to understand that Satanism is

The Occult Compendium

not a harmful, warlike, insane ideology (in fact, Satanism, unlike most other religions people practice, directly attempts to prohibit things like child abuse and animal abuse, which is not only seemingly tolerated in christianity and islam, but sometimes even commanded.) We will call this admonishment the *quasi-pacifistic admonishment.*

In the case where individuals do not understand or apply the first concept, they tend to gravitate over time further from Satanism, not truly realizing their own sovereign state- in the case where they do not understand or apply the second, they become mere egotists, not truly elite in any realistic sense, because they are in fact enslaved to their senses to the point where they destroy themselves, and in the case where they do not understand or apply the third concept, all too often they end up drawn into dangerous cults, or become addicts, or otherwise destroy themselves or others through their own misinterpretation of what was originally a very positive philosophy.

So here we must reject, in the conventional sense, elitism, and instead redefine it; for elitism in a Satanic sense does not mean merely preserving the self and building the ego, but being smart enough to control it, and self controlled

The Occult Compendium

enough not to use ones' own skills to usurp others, often to one's own simultaneous detriment.

Instead, we must redefine elitism as a combination of skills, self control, and intelligence (either innate or gained.) It is entirely possible for a person to, in essence, "convert" to Satanism if given the right skills to do so- something which not all Satanists can or will be willing to apply themselves to, but which others, at their own leisure, may choose to do.

The world today has become a sort of quagmire- a combination of often violent reactionary sentiment, and often delusional progressive sentiment, overseen by political parties, businesses, and other organized groups which seek to fool the general population, in an effort to gain money and power; and while Satanism was originally founded with certain psychological and social concepts in mind (and might in a way be seen as a roughly Jeffersonian philosophy at its core) it seems to have at least in part succumbed to this same tendency, in essence that disorganized groups of Satanists more or less continued to understand the philosophy while organized groups became little more than fronts to sell merchandise and memberships.

The Occult Compendium

There are only two roads which Satanism can travel- the first is to remain more or less underground, more or less unappreciated and unused by the general population, and more or less inactive when it comes to the way in which society runs- the second, that it should seek to grow, gain more power, and exert its own collective force on the world.

In this modern age, there is great danger to every liberty-loving philosophy, and Satanism is among these endangered species; for more and more governments and societies, especially in the increasingly politically correct western world and the increasingly fascist asian region, are using a combination of surveillance, censorship, and hostile takeover of all communication sources to grind their populations down and attempt to prevent people from spreading what the mainstream culture considers "bad" messages.

A person could write thousands of pages alone on the inherent dangers of these movements, that there could come a day when it is virtually impossible to have a world in which Satanism can even exist, because it could be labeled a cult, or

The Occult Compendium

a dangerous and subversive political minority- once this time comes, in any given culture, the Satanist will either submit to slavery or flee to greener lands, with their home culture destroyed either by totalitarian leftists and their delusional and self hating political correctness, or totalitarian reactionaries, which will march brownshirts through the streets, or possibly the rise of quasi-theocracy in which only the majority religious group is truly tolerated, with Satanism likely relegated to the "vile heathen" tier and abused continuously.

What LaVey and almost every other Satanist in the past has overlooked, is that the principle of "Might is Right" extends to the society at large- it is not just a struggle involving the individual, but in some cases (including the same revolutions that brought western plurality into birth) can involve the upheaval of an entire nation, or multiple nations, as they seek to restore some semblance of peace and tolerance to their lands. If the Satanic communist is unwilling to use every means possible to preserve itself, it will die out and be forgotten, as all other cultures, religions, languages, and nations, have gone extinct when they are usurped by a more aggressively self preserving outside culture, or religion, or language, or nation; this is a well-

The Occult Compendium

understood concept, that cannot be denied, and which anyone with a casual understanding of history or anthropology can understand. It comes down to the pure equation of life, that things which do not fight to preserve themselves, or change over time and adapt to persevere, are eventually destroyed and replaced- but it is possible, with a sort of Satanic "reformation" for this philosophy to not only continue to exist and perpetuate liberty and freedom, but also to grow in size, in power, and to replace other, less powerful groups along the way, eventually securing its place in the western world at large and perhaps further over time, creating waves of liberation movements even in the most despotic nations.

The manner in which this is to be done is in understanding how the Satanic philosophy itself is able to mesh with collective will and with collective idealism- in many cases, because as I stated before, Satanists are egotists without a greater understanding of the world, they see no particular reason to perpetuate the ideology, because their philosophy (which isn't even truly Satanic in form) is merely "I have mine, and damn the rest."

This self destructive philosophy eventually weeds

itself out and forms the basis for every villain in mythology and legend, the basis for every sappy movie that involves a damsel in distress, or a village being sacked by goblins or knights in black armor- it is not possible in a fully dynamic, darwinistic, selective, and evolving world, for such an ideology to grow in size, and often even for it to continue existing for very long before more well organized groups subvert it.

Thus the answer is in understanding; for while the ego and selfishness are central to Satanic philosophy, it is in the second concept that allows Satanism to flex its collective strength when necessary- for Satanists possessing the ability of truly rational thought, of common sense, will see that the words here are true, and will begin to organize and spread, like the scales of a snake retracting inwards as it grows, forming its armor, preserving it against attack- Satanism, to survive, must consist not just of mindless egotists obsessed with their own sexuality and gain of wealth, but must also contain organizers, the intelligent, the strong, the strong-wiled, the charismatic, and people from every walk of life, who are united, perhaps solely, by their belief in individualism and freedom; this is why it is true, when I say that Satanism, at its most simple, is *merely an extension of*

The Occult Compendium

rational, and mostly libertarian, Jeffersonian philosophy.
Even LaVey, when he wrote the Satanic Bible, based his writings on Ragnar Redbeards' "Might is Right" which is itself mostly a manifesto revolving around the types of early 1900s philosophies that echoed Jefferson and forsook Rand or Marx.

Satanism is not the same as pure egotism- pure egotism isn't even particularly freedom loving in reality, since it encourages (actively or passively) individuals to seek to reduce the freedom of others, siphoning their wealth and vigor at their expense, and at the hazard of the one doing the siphoning, should the other party decide to take some sort of revenge- such petty ways have destroyed nations, never created wealth or freedom, and end up, after a time, becoming the antithesis of a Satanic society, eventually withering on the vine like spoiled fruit, removing the opportunity of those residing therein to prosper, or in extreme cases, to survive.

Take, for example, North Korea, which today we can say is not only radically and diametrically opposed to the western ethos at large, but which is so absolutely authoritarian that the slightest infraction against traditionalist

The Occult Compendium

law can cause a citizen thereof to be hung or shot or fed to starving animals.

This perpetually nonsensical land, in which there are stores full of goods that aren't for sale, and in which the ground is slowly being eroded by intensified agriculture, which will eventually result in not just famine but utter depopulation, was originally founded by individuals who wished to resist what they saw as an imperialistic western incursion into their way of life- unfortunately for these individuals, who died by the thousands trying to defend their piece of land, those that ended up seizing control after their war turned out to be far, far worse than the supposed imperialists they were fighting, and as a result many of their more talented individuals were killed during the war or in the ethnic purge thereafter- thus North Korea sits, isolated, impoverished, and lacking even basic amenities.

Had the North Koreans understood the concept of individual sovereignty, they might not just be a solvent and free nation, but perhaps among the richest- the land they hold is rich with minerals and fuel resources, which have only begun to be extracted, yet the majority of their population remains malnourished and under the boots of

The Occult Compendium

their government, because the population forgot that after fighting the foreign armies was done, as is the case in all wars on domestic soil, they should have kept fighting their own internal demons as well- it is possible to establish a nationalist, even traditionalist state, that remains inclusive of a mostly libertarian way of life- a fusion model which, while not outright Satanic in form, at least preserves the better part of its vision.

So too will the fate be for all of the world if those who value freedom above state protection, and selfish action above collective group welfare, cease to organize, cease to fight for their beliefs (mainly on a ideological scale, although physical conflict is sometimes, unfortunately, inevitable.)

Right now, as we speak, incursions by theocracy in the middle east is a rising threat to the true values of liberty and individualism- islam is a dangerous, violent ideology, for even while its more liberal adherents adapt to a western lifestyle, when we observe the things said in their hadiths and quran, we can see that taking it too literally (especially out of context as some do) can spawn extremist groups with relative ease, even when compared to christianity.

The Occult Compendium

In the west the situation is not much better- the rise of censorship and acceptance of political correctness is a threat to free speech and expression, with some nations in Europe going so far as to use or propose to use the justice system to suppress the views of groups they deem inappropriate, even when in some cases these groups are no more "extreme" than groups which would be considered part of the mainstream in other fully western nations- political correctness is more of a bane to freedom than theocracy, because theocracy does not pretend to be freedom loving and admits its own somewhat totalitarian tendencies, while the purveyors of political correctness disguise their fascism (for it can only be enforced by the state) as a freedom loving form of tolerance that invites criticism, while in reality it attempts to use emotional fallacies to squash any dissent, branding itself as tolerant while remaining intolerant to viewpoints counter to its activities.

In other regions of the world a form of resurgent nationalism has become the main threat to liberty- and nationalism is a special case- for while theocracy, based on the illogical notions of religious cultism, and political correctness, based on irrational emotional arguments, are both inherently opposed to liberty, nationalism is not

The Occult Compendium

necessarily so, unless destroying dissent is made part of their nationalistic platform.

So for every Stalinist takeover, which results in millions of casualties, a nationalistic and democratic state such as Switzerland (which by and large has been one of the least authoritarian and most tolerant states in history while preserving its cultural heritage) can arise- and while the former results in misery and destruction, the latter tends to be wealthy and at least tolerably free, allowing its people a great deal of flexibility in how they choose to run their state.

Very few states, in the current time period, are becoming more free, and this is due to a multitude of factors, not least among them being the tendency of growing government to eventually reach such a mass that it begins to hide its actions in red tape, thousand page long laws, and closed door meetings, consulting business heads and lobbyists rather than panels actually representing real, living, breathing citizens.

There is hope, however, for freedom, and for the Satanic way of life- a few states have shaken off this tendency and are moving towards greater liberty and away from the

The Occult Compendium

paranoid totalitarianism of aggressive statism as is the case in parts of Europe and the insanity of theocracy in other areas-certain middle eastern states have long resisted islamism, such as Tunisia or Turkey, and have built for themselves secularity which has made them, in comparison to their neighbors, wealthy and prosperous-and here in the United States, the exposure of government corruption to public scrutiny, particularly with regards to domestic surveillance, has reignited a fervorous move towards libertarianism-which has manifested in the growth of the vote dedicated to the actual libertarian party at an exponential level, which, if it continues, might cause it to gain major party status- no small feat for a party that was once largely unknown to exist by the majority of the population. And while I have my misgivings about this party and its affiliation with certain christian moralists, it is at least better than the so-called grand old party or their progressive enemies on the other side of the aisle.

In France, a growing number of people have begun to embrace their old motto of "liberty, brotherhood, equality" and have called for the government to relinquish its grasp on their wallets and minds, and in Britain, increasing numbers of people are migrating to political fronts which

The Occult Compendium

seek to put the British first, and to curtail the islamist immigration which is destabilizing their nation.

However, for each of these successes, there is at least one loss- the christian churches have begun to push heavily in Africa, attempting to stall out the expansion of islam, and themselves making the lives of the affected almost as bad as if the shariah law supporters had dominated them- that the church pays tribute to freedom here in the west while propping up theocracy-lite in Africa has always amused me, and probably amuses other people, who can only look on in amazement at the hypocrisy.

There was once a time, many years ago, when the western man attempted to perfect the world- at the dawn of the industrial revolution, an explosion of literature and philosophy and education, of reform and conquest, seemed to herald the coming singularity at which the entire world would eventually become ordered and free- this moderately open-minded Victorian sentiment only began to break down as the now increasingly powerful colonial states began to quibble amongst themselves over disputed land, and to mistreat the people which were present in lands outside of their European or American cores; the biggest mistake the

The Occult Compendium

western world ever made, was to infight amongst themselves and attempt to abuse native populations (which often had far larger populations than they could manage) and to eventually give up these colonial lands, rather than to attempt to educate the people they encountered and to perpetuate secular and pluralist values– had they done so, it's entirely possible both world wars could have been avoided.

The ultimate Satanic dream, would thus be a world of liberty and freedom, in which totalitarianism has been relegated to a brief chapter in history books on failed states, and in which theocracy has been shunned by an ever more literate population in favor of plurality, tolerance of differences at the same time that each culture preserves its heritage– the libertarians have told people for decades that a good foreign policy is to leave others alone insofar as it is possible and use rewards or incentives to change their posturing rather than to attack or belittle foreigners– in this they have shown great intelligence, even as the majority of the population clamors for ever more weapons, which grow more expensive by the day, in hopes that eventually, their nation and no other will reign supreme– failing to realize that if this happens, the government possessing such power will have free reign to usher in a world of tyrants and puppet leaders.

In short, elitism, regarded as mindless egotism, and the resultant stagnation of the Satanic philosophy, which should be attempting to both aid and alter libertarian philosophy, constitutionalism, and all individualistic organizations and groups, could in time sound the death knell of not only Satanism as an ideology, but also liberty itself. It is not alarmism, a conspiracy theory, or an unlikely worst-case scenario rant to state that the world is in great danger, at this present moment, because for many decades people have largely been herded into political groups and organizations which do not truly represent western values, but have adopted a variety of theocratic and generally authoritarian leanings.

THE BIRTH OF THE ADEPT

Becoming a Satanist is far easier than most people believe- in my own activities, I have taught many hundreds, possibly thousands of people about Satanism, what it means, and how to practice it- an activity that I enjoy, and which I employ in part to make amends for my time spent as a

The Occult Compendium

deluded and marginally theocratic christian.

The majority of the population already has one of the three stated qualities of Satanism which I have already covered- in the western world, egotism is already rife (which is a large and growing social problem leading to more harm than good on its own) while in the eastern world, where buddhism, daoism, and hinduism encourage a sapphic lifestyle, the concept of not harming others is common, but egotism is shunned.

In either case, an imbalance is created- the western human is most often concerned only with themselves, with monetary gain, comfort- a narcissistic and sometimes sociopathic behavior which causes inequity- and not the acceptable inequity which drives progress, but the systematic, almost impossibly bloated inequity of status that prevents upward mobility and prevents even talented individuals, in many cases, from reaching their full potential.

The eastern human is most often concerned with a sort of irrational hatred of materialism, to the point where when authoritarians take over, the average pacifistic buddhist or sapphic hindu doesn't care, because they believe that their

The Occult Compendium

own flesh is sinful and fallen; oddly, christianity teaches this very concept, but this concept has been abandoned in favor of the hypocritical church of the golden cross where the preacher sits on a silk lined throne screaming about humility, then drives away from the service in a limousine.

    The trifecta is completed when we consider the nihilistic state of modern science with its overarching hatred for anything that does not conform to a consensus, peer reviewed state; long gone are the days where a crazy-haired sort of self taught mad scientist might discover a cure for cancer in his basement, long gone are the Teslas and Einsteins, who either shunned academia and did their own work separate from the white towers of education, or who shunned society to the point where they might be considered psychopathic, involved only with blind ambition to innovate.

    Modern science has almost become a sort of religion- one of the few concepts which the evangelical christians are correct about (albeit for the wrong reasons.) Science has become politicized, to the point where views outside the mainstream are relegated to the back row and labeled loony ramblings or fringe pseudoscience, even where a theory has

The Occult Compendium

been concocted which is at least logically consistent.

The insistence on pure secularity and upon ruthless use of logic in the absence of any egotistical enjoyment, and especially if respect for human life and value is lacking, has crippled modern science, which in the days of old at least enjoyed a flirtatious relationship with the mystic and with the fringe, where human life was made at least more interesting and at best much more enjoyable by tales, whether true or false, of buried treasure or of the discovery of some ancient burial site which sits undisturbed because of ancient curses of darkness and the infernal.

How often has science been criticized because it persists in harming animals in its search for immortality and health, and how often has it all but ignored even somewhat substantiated fringe claims because of the horror it experiences when faced with the possibility that its prior convictions may be wrong? Physics and engineering continues to churn out new innovations every day, while the more theoretical side of science has stagnated into a cesspit of hallowed tradition and unspoken regulation, which all but invalidates its very existence- theoretical science seems to have had its heyday around the 1950s, and has

The Occult Compendium

declined ever since.

Thus, the birth of the Satanist is rooted in the fusion of these traits, at least one of which is held by, I believe, every human being on earth- from the self obsessed westerner, to the mystic easterner, and even into the already elitist halls of science and advancement itself.

That is to say, in essence, that these three qualities on their own are debased, at least to an extent where they become extreme in their use, whereas when they are all present together, a certain nobility arises, and a certain respect for dignity and liberty is able to manifest- let us remember that those who founded what is now pluralistic western philosophy, namely certain French and Revolutionary American figures, were themselves purveyors of all three, creating their success through this fusion.

The founders of the United States, or the French revolutionaries, were themselves quite egotistical- enough so that they were willing to behead members of their own government, and seek their own pleasure of representation, and they were surely logical and rational, many of them authors and visionaries, inventors and leaders through both

The Occult Compendium

?ed. Moreover, these figures fairly obviously
d peace and attempted to preserve it, for even when they eventually resorted to warfare and rebellion, they first attempted to gain their liberty through words, education, and by petition.

The birth of Satanism in the mind of one of its ideological adherents (regardless of their own beliefs with regards to theism versus atheism, for there are both within Satanism) sometimes begins with a sort of traumatic sudden recognition that their preconceived notions of reality are wrong, or in the case where they have been taught a sort of fanatic absolutism, this trauma may be caused by even a slight nagging feeling that their belief even *might* be wrong.

In some cases, this can take the form of academia- whereby the individual begins to study comparative religion, anthropology, or some other field. To the sheltered mind of an evangelical faced with insurmountable evidence that the world is not 6,000 years old and that at least half of the bible they read was adapted from other cultures and religious groups outside of judeochristianity, this knowledge is a sort of arcana- a forbidden fruit of sorts that they more often than not begin to gobble down greedily, realizing this is the

The Occult Compendium

spiritual content which their former faith never gave them- for how much more powerful and desirable is truth and knowledge, when compared to the comforting but obvious lies of their former path?

In other cases, the entry into Satanism might be aided by the home life- abusive fundamentalist parents, or sexual abuse at the hands of family or clergy- we see this rampant sexual perversion all too often in orthodox judaism and catholicism especially, as well as most of the arabian schools of islam, where children are relegated to the status of objects, or where abusing them is considered less sinful or not a sin at all, either within their teachings or in the deranged minds of the individual clergymembers- and especially with catholicism, perverts are drawn like moths to an open flame, because of the twofold guarantee of the church- first that it promises to heal them of their guilt, and secondly because its massive stockpile of ready cash all but ensures that even the worst offenders get off scott free. We need look no further than a jewish mohel sucking the freshly circumcised member of an infant, or any of the more notorious priests and imams with their young male counterparts to understand the wickedness and perversion of these churches. These same bodies proclaim themselves to be holy and all other groups

The Occult Compendium

to be evil, even as they themselves perpetuate the most evil of deeds.

I myself have known many former christians and children raised in evangelical families, who have left their faith due to any combination of physical or sexual abuse, systemic perversion at the clerical level, or general disdain for their former faith once they are exposed to a little bit of actual historical knowledge- churches attempt to prevent this by deliberately skipping over pieces of the quran or bible or talmud that are nonsensical in a modern context, or which are blatantly evil and vile, so that the younger, usually more astute members of their congregations do not ask too many questions.

If you spend enough time on the internet you will eventually meet the wiccan who left a protestant life because they were raped, a former muslim living in Arabia who knows he can be stoned for becoming an apostate, and you'll meet many young men and women, some as young as their early teens or even younger, who are being raised as christians, jews, and muslims, but who do not believe in their gods and are inwardly hostile towards their own family and the congregation they're forced to be part of.

The Occult Compendium

As far as the typical left-right politics of the United States and certain other western nations are concerned, there is an element of Satanic philosophy in both sides- taking the example of the two major parties in the United States, we see a Democratic party which sides squarely with a Satanic worldview when it comes to issues such as abortion and gay marriage, seeking to make or keep such things legal, at the same time that they also espouse a quasi-Satanic view of environmentalism. At the same time, we have a Republican party that has at least some level of Satanic continuity when it comes to the free market, or the right to keep and bear arms- this explains why Satanists fall on both sides as well as in the middle, with some, myself included, exempting themselves from this and designating their own views irrespective of party affiliation or ideology.

Satan, and of course Satanism along with this figure, is always used as the standard *de facto* villain when one group wishes to demonize another using false emotional appeals- for example, "Bush is Satan" or "That group that I don't like is no better than a bunch of devil worshipers." Satanism has replaced the term "witch" largely in the public lexicon, just like pre-1940s language revolved around egging

The Occult Compendium

on ones' enemies by likening them to Napoleon or Benedict Arnold, with these terms then replaced by Hitler and, to an extent later on, Charles Manson.

The birth of Satanism in an individual may thus sometimes be the result of disaffection towards society as a whole, with its often inane and confusing lexicon of terms- the desensitization of the public towards Satan and its embracing of this figure as part of pop culture has perpetuated Satanism to a certain extent. In truth, Satanism has only begun to be accepted as anything other than a dangerous occult ideology of great malevolence, because the generation which perpetuated the Satanic Panic (Burning Times 2, the Return of Paranoia) has only begun to grow old and die off, leaving their heavy metal loving children with Ouija boards in their wake- oddly the soccer moms of the 1980s, the children of hippies, were less tolerant of alternative lifestyles than their parents had been.

The new generation has the added advantage of a vast playground called the internet- something which did not exist in public use when LaVey wrote his own work, and much less so when Lord Byron waxed poetic about Lucifer in his own works many years before- those were the

The Occult Compendium

days of vinyl albums and psychedelic music. In the modern age, a far greater scope of material is available to the youth on the largely (at least for now) free and uncensored internet, where virtually any poem, book, song, or movie is instantly available for perusal, in which it is possible to speak with people on the other side of the planet in real time- this information exchange has resulted in a far less limited world, where the well established darwinistic nature of human ideology has begun to weed out fundamentalism and abrahamism, resulting in the drastic growth of groups ranging from hedge wicca, to Satanism, through neopaganism and new age movements. In the modern sense, a group which back in the 1960s would have remained a local commune with a dozen members, can now grow at its leisure, as long as its ideas are regarded as worth practicing by outsiders who see the information they make publicly available.

The youth is the key to Satanism's growth. Amusingly, if these words reach the ears of christian ministries, they will point to this very passage and remark "aha, I knew these devil worshiping miscreants want to destroy the youth!"

The Occult Compendium

However, they are blind to their own negative impact on the young, through the perversion of their teachings and actions, a disgusting ensemble of lies and mistreatment which in the past has led to genocide and mass murder through hysteria and paranoia, the natural results of unstable minds filled with fanciful nonsense. Satanism seeks to liberate the same youth that they lie to, by reminding them that those churches they went to, that told them they were vile and fallen beings, are wrong, and that it is society itself, not they as individuals, who are dysfunctional- that they can re-balance and improve their lives with fairly little effort by merely ignoring the idiocy of the pulpit and the state it tries to control.

Satanism opposes lies- and the same secularists that constantly ask "Why believe in Satan? that's as bad as christianity!" don't seem to understand that a majority of Satanists are atheists and apatheists and either do not believe in a literal Satan, or do not care about theism one way or the other. On this count, the atheists at large show little more understanding of the topic than the christians do.

Sexuality can also be a potent wake-up call for the soon-to-be Satanist.

The Occult Compendium

Most churches, especially the christian and islamic ones, teach that human sexuality is a low, denigrating, horrifically ugly thing- that only in the realm of marriage, and often solely for the purpose of procreating, is sexuality anything other than debased and condemned. They do this in order to exert control over their laypeople, literally attempting to monopolize on the most natural instinctual behavior of them all.

These wild-faced stump preachers who try to shame teenagers into taking vows of celibacy are utter morons- for human sexuality, long ago, before the perverts took over and founded judaism and its ever more crazy offshoots, was seen as it should be, as a blessed force, a wonderful passtime, and something that should not only be regarded as positive, but something also that should have entire stories dedicated to the topic.

In many ways, the move towards sexualizing pop culture can be seen not so much as a degradation from western tradition but a restoration of the true western traditions rooted in ancient Greece- the western world spent many centuries in the hands of cultures that thought

The Occult Compendium

sexuality to be not just normal and tolerable but something to be spoken of openly and celebrated, sometimes with elaborate religious rituals, orgies, and so forth- this is the true history of the western, civilized world, the true history of the bohemian pastoralist.

Thankfully, in this regard, the fanatics are destroying themselves almost more effectively than any outside force could possibly do them damage. Teenagers will always have sex, no matter how many moral strictures or laws are used, and people will always have premarital sex- the church could assert utter theocracy and begin beheading adulterers and premaritally promiscuous individuals, and it would still happen, and this would eventually do what it did before and lead to a libertine awakening which would be, to the theocrats' mind, even more debasing and vile than the sexual revolution we see today.

And these same churches and preachers and politicians, who spend the majority of their time worrying about others who have more sexual contact in a month than they have in their entire lives, have the gall to rant about how birth control causes sexual promiscuity, even in the same breath that they condemn abortion, which any sane

The Occult Compendium

individual knows becomes less common when contr... is more widely available. In the same breath that they make their feeble arguments for regulating abortion, these same imbeciles proclaim that sexual education, when taught, should revolve heavily around the topic of abstinence, which has never worked in the history of humankind, never will work in the future, and only causes more pregnancy, which is then often taken care of at an abortion clinic.

One might even think that the most moneygrubbing and dishonest amongst them actually know that this is the case, and say these things on purpose, with the goal of making abortion more prevalent so they can continue to use it as an emotional wedge issue during election years- nothing is too vile, sickening, perverted, and dishonest, to come from any pulpit in the western world, where the sexually vile priest or pastor or imam will hypocritically tell his flock how bad extra-marital affairs are, while secretly lusting for the young ladies in the front row with the low-cut blouses.

The nature of the human being is sexual, egotistical, nature-loving, and intellectually curious- this is the true sentience of the human race.

The Occult Compendium

This is the reason why groups which embrace these values are growing quickly- atheists embrace the intellect, Pagans embrace the natural, Satanists embrace the ego, and all of the above more or less embrace the sexual, casting off the strictures and lies of the abrahamist groups. Paganism alone is growing so quickly that certain European nations might soon legitimately see actual pagan revivalist parties running for office, and the occult and mystic never really died out in this world and never will, only going underground temporarily to resist persecution, which rears its head from time to time.

I am of the mind, having studied the statistics involved where possible, and having inferred a probable result, that quite a large minority and perhaps even a small majority of self-proclaimed christians, muslims, and jews, don't even believe in their own god, and question its existence constantly, while at the same time largely ignoring their religions' teachings. This can be seen as a good thing on one hand because these individuals may resist the paranoia that others embrace, while it can also be negative at times, because when trauma hits, they might become the most fundamentalist of all adherents.

The Occult Compendium

An individual may also choose to study Satanism on the basis that it is "cool." On this I can issue one part blessing and one part warning, for while it is good to study Satanism, it's not necessarily a good idea to join its ideological core simply because it appears to be interesting or hold some sort of special status- it is a philosophy like many others, and while those of us who adhere to this philosophy feel it is more intellectually and spiritually advanced than, and superior to, other philosophies, it must be understood in order to be used to any great effect in ones' life.

The likening of Satanism with, for example, heavy metal, or gothic culture, or other phenomena, is only partially true, and the "coolness" of Satanism to a certain subset of the youth often seems to go hand in hand with its peripheral relation with these other groups. It is true, for example, that quite a few musicians within metal (especially black metal) are Satanists, either theistic or atheistic, and it is true that gothic music and culture does borrow from similar themes as Satanism, but if you look deeper, a lot of the earlier musicians and authors and other folks involved with actual Satanism were producing ambient music, or writing philosophical tracts, or were artists and photographers-

The Occult Compendium

Anton LaVey himself released music, and most of it would fall roughly in the category of circus themed or classical music, certainly not heavy metal.

However, here we might see more of Satanism's influence, since it spawned so many styles and themes within musical and literary circles- many thousands of musical acts are either conducted by Satanists themselves or contain references to the ideology, or to styles popularized in the 1960s by LaVey, or in the 1980s by associated groups such as NON or Radio Werewolf- the dominance of Satanism in some of these circles, and later of pagan groups which included Satanic elements in their work, has been worrying to the church and its allies. Mostly, the churches fear what they do not understand- their belief is that Satanism and other non-abrahamic groups are growing in both size and influence mainly because they also believe that Satan is real, very much evil, and asserting his own mystical control over the population, especially through pop music, which has garnered a great deal of attention from both mainstream clergy as well as fringe conspiracy theorists. Their theories cause many chuckles in the actual Satanic community though, because they're often so deluded they are more bad joke than reality.

The Occult Compendium

In fact, one of the few things holding Satanism back from reaching out to tens of millions of people, is that the largest Satanic organization (the Church of Satan, originally founded by LaVey but now run by others in the wake of his death) doesn't seem up to the task of actually organizing anything, which has forced dozens of smaller groups to do the actual real-life work.

Individuals may also be drawn to Satanism because of the work of individual Satanists in the world, work which they may relate to- this has brought large groups into Satanic ideologies which range from very close to the original philosophy to somewhat warped interpretations thereof- the claim of the mass media that Charles Manson was a Satanist (which was never actually the case) ended up bringing thousands of neonazis into the philosophy, believing that he had created a sort of Hitleresque fusion of nazi occultism with his own supposed demonic powers.

In a way, the same partisan political and theological bodies that brand their enemies with Satanic insults, are just causing more individuals to study the philosophy, which necessarily results in some of them adopting it as their own-

The Occult Compendium

in fact, in typical psychological fashion, whatever the mass media brands as evil just ends up being adopted by rebellious young people as good, seeking to usurp the reigning society. One can imagine a ten year old hearing that their favorite fictional series is evil and Satanic because it references witchcraft, then going onto the internet, looking up Satanism, and realizing it is both appealing and positive, and thus begins their secret double life- a churchgoing child on the outside, and the deep seated internal psychology of a liberated individual, who is even too young to vote.

Oddly, the church, the media, and the politicians, do not see the danger or irony in attempting to censor, ban, and destroy the Satanic ideology, while at the same time claiming that society has been infected with rampant Satanism- if this is truly the case, one would think they would not want to set a legal precedent for banning it, and would worry that if they did, Satanists might take over and in turn censor and harass them. In this token, we can say for certain that their paranoid references to rampant Satanism and witchcraft are meant to frighten suburban soccer moms and thus extract money for exorcisms, prayer lines, and votes.

It is important for Satanic individuals to cultivate

The Occult Compendium

their skills– some individuals, depressed because of society and perhaps those around them, actively cultivate an aura of hopelessness, as though they did not matter, at times because others have told them so; in these cases, depression can be alleviated when the individual observes that those around them are at best their equals and at times far inferior, and that their feelings of isolation and hopelessness are not worth having, because their own aptitude is theirs, mostly, to determine, and all individuals possess skills and talents that they can use to advance their own lot in life.

Satanism is most often seen as related to music, art, and philosophy, since these particular skills tend to draw high visibility especially when associated with any alternative religious path. It would be strange, though, to ignore the sometimes less visible but equally potent skills of others, who may work at a completely "normal" job by day, or they may be self employed, or independently wealthy and do other work. The best advice that can be given to the depressed, especially to the youth, who wish to free themselves of the bondage of negativity derived from religions and from society, is to attempt to focus on what they themselves feel they do well, and use their brain to figure out how it can become profitable and useful in their lives.

The Occult Compendium

ever, all of this being said, the birth of the Satanist does not truly come until after they assert dominance over their own existence. This assertion does not necessarily take the form of mindless rebellion, or of becoming a hermit and exempting oneself from all authority, but more often (and with better results) takes the result of a psychological subversion of the reigning cultural and religious phenomena of the society itself- an internal decision to forsake both, and adhere to a Satanic ideology. An individual can live in society and be part of it, while still being their own master, even if they are working for their boss or listening to their parents, because their mind, ultimately, and their thoughts and dreams, are their own, free of all censorship and control by others.

Once the mind is free, the body follows suit- perhaps it is dangerous to believe this, but within the scope of Satanic philosophy, all unjust laws are essentially null and void, especially when legalism crawls more slowly than societal consciousness. We see this to be the case with, say, drug law and laws involving free speech, where society has largely now come to the conclusion that in the former case most nonviolent "offenders" should be released and not jailed for

The Occult Compendium

the "crime" they commit, while in the latter case, society has largely determined that the government should take a hands off approach especially with regards to electronic communication.

The adept will need to determine for themselves what the right course of action is- this can be difficult especially for those who have gotten used to getting their morals from external and often antiquated sources such as the bible or quran. In this intermediate period, where they are free but confused, it is possible that they will become frightened and return to slavery rather than continue to dwell in freedom, hence the importance in more seasoned individuals giving them aid when they are willing to do so- some individuals wish to do so, and some do not, and in either case that too is their own decision. Those of us who have benefited from encountering, early on, Satanists who were both willing and able to discuss the philosophy, tend to remain within its ideology, while those who do not have this benefit given to them tend to become confused, because at the same time that the church and media tell them that Satanism is evil, groups which call themselves Satanic but are actually following utterly different philosophies will try to draft these individuals into their ranks for their own benefit

The Occult Compendium

(which is usually monetary in nature.)

On this the christians have their story half right- every time someone gets jailed for mass murder they seem to tell the same "Satan made me do it" crocodile tear story, as though the red man with a pitchfork himself was conjured before them in a puff of smoke, telling them to slaughter other human beings, or sacrifice animals to the infernal. These individuals are invariably *not* members of any truly Satanic organization, nor do they actually follow a Satanic philosophy. Instead, this is an example of either psychosis, lying, or cults that refer to themselves as Satanists or Luciferians, but which are not.

In the former cases, individuals who have been caught and face lengthy prison sentences, will often resort to the last ditch hope of being declared insane on the basis that they are hallucinating demons and devils, or their claim of possession is meant to hopefully sway the jury, in the hopes that at least one member is superstitious enough to take them seriously, causing a mistrial. In the less common latter case, the individual may have been part of an actual violent cult, which really does command ritual murder or animal abuse- the new Satanist needs to know to avoid any groups which

The Occult Compendium

have such teachings, or which seem to be acting in a psychologically unhealthy manner, although such cults are typically rare, and many don't welcome new members anyways.

It is not possible to prescribe a method, either for the Satanic community or new Satanists, to prevent every case where someone ends up abandoning the philosophy because they were deluded by a cult or the media- however, there is a grain of happiness here anyways, because such individuals rarely return to judeochristianity (despite a handful of fluff stories presented by evangelicals, only a minority of which are even authentic cases of reconversion) and instead seem to make their way into the occult or into secular atheism or paganism, groups which, if not directly Satanic in sum, are at the very least far more positive and worthy of respect than the hypocritical christians, muslims, and jews who rule the world.

The would-be Satanist is also advised that, despite claims to the contrary that are repeated daily in every church and mosque, the vast majority of powerful individuals, politicians, and media heads in the western world are abrahamists. This is a fact that is slightly obscured by the

The Occult Compendium

right and left wing groups attacking each other, often attempting to liken the other side with some sort of fanaticism, often of a religious nature (the left wing is, in the United States, especially fond of claiming that its ideological enemies are all fanatic evangelicals, which is not always the case.) The counter used by the right wing is thus that their opponents lack religion or religious fervor, which seems odd since every major candidate who runs in the entire party seems to be a christian or a jew.

Outside of the west it's even worse, with religion not just philosophically intertwined with the political system but actually a mandated portion of it, with the islamists and hindus at the forefront of legislating based on religious morals- the adept needs to be aware that this is the case, and not fall for the often repeated lie that the world is fallen into Satanism and secularity with religion in steep decline. Yes, abrahamism is in steep decline as a proportion of the population, and is losing favor with both the youth and disaffected minority groups, but it is still very much the dominant force in western and eastern politics, with alternative religious and ideological forces barely being tolerated even in fully developed nations- it wasn't long ago that Satanism all but disappeared underground for fear of a

The Occult Compendium

very real, physical reprisal by millions of evangelicals, and it wasn't long ago that individuals were being given electroshock therapy in mental wards because they left their families' religion and said they did not believe in god.

It is my own personal belief, that anyone who wishes to become a Satanist, should study anthropology and history- both ancient and modern- from as many cultures and backgrounds as they can find. This is solely my own opinion, and surely there are those with little interest in these subjects, but a broad overview of these academic topics will arm the Satanist with an enormous amount of knowledge related to religion and culture. However, it should be noted that as stated before, the scientific community at large tends to be unaccepting of theories outside the mainstream, so it is prudent to study counter-arguments and counter-theories to any theory studied, even if those counters are considered fringe views by the mainstream of science.

The Occult Compendium

BREAK THE TABOO

One of the more important aspects of Satanism, that I have myself realized, is its psychological prowess, and its ability to deprogram individuals who have been indoctrinated into various severities of guilt and fear courtesy of, mostly, christian religion. The guilt and fear associated with tales of Santa Claus may be seen as a sort of transitional period before the child is told that god, not Santa, is the one watching them, and instead of coal in the stocking, this being is far more evil, and prefers to rake sinners over hot coals eternally.

Satanism has the unique ability to replace these feelings of guilt and fear with those of self empowerment and ambition- this is perhaps its most important aspect, for it invites philosophy and logic to be used within an indoctrinated individuals' life, so that instead of, say, them joining a different religion that is simply less judgmental (the newer religion saves them from those feelings externally) Satanism allows them to instead save themselves, ripping those cancerous ideologies out of their head entirely.

The Occult Compendium

I, too, was raised christian, and indoctrinated into the usual mumbo-jumbo of worrying whether god was watching me when I had sex, or had impure thoughts, or committed other sins- most individuals in the world are the same, being told over and over at a young age that everything they are told to do is because of god or jesus or some angel or saint, and that to disobey is to risk hellfire- what a good way to raise generations of slaves that will gladly deal with whatever abuse is heaped upon them, for they will blame themselves; the outcome is a population that resembles one in which every relationship includes an aspect of ritualized domestic abuse.

It isn't enough to simply leave the religion and stop believing in the deity; only for some people does this do anything other than leave them constantly fearful that they have made the wrong decision and are now hellbound sinners; the guilt and fear spread by abrahamism is powerful, hence why it has existed for so long and only recently begun to decline and lose power because of more positive, less arcane religious groups. In order to expunge the mind totally of this sort of nagging worrying, Satanism is able to prescribe a simple process, which is roughly equivalent to certain teachings found within (but applied differently) among some

The Occult Compendium

pagan groups, particularly within tantric circles, and within certain mystic or ancient cults.

The process is simply the breaking of the taboo- a powerful statement of self awareness and self choice that is even utilized by those in extremely strict ascetic schools of thought, whereby they may abstain, for example, from meat, alcohol, sex, or other desirable things for a long period of time. In many of these cases, it takes the form of a ritual, which may be yearly, or otherwise, in which vows taken as part of the ascetic tradition are deliberately broken, in a reverent and conscientious manner. In these cases, the goal is to show that the same restraint applied to everyday life (the giving up of materialism, or sexuality, or whatever else has been discarded with regularity and shunned) can also be restrained to the ascetic lifestyle itself, such that the individual remains sovereign. In this, the notion is that if the individual is *not ever able* under any circumstances, to *ever* break their vows, they aren't even truly conscientious and are automatons, unable to truly be classed as ascetics, because this lifestyle must be chosen deliberately; the member thus shows that they are able at any time to revert to materialism and sexuality, but that they are choosing not to and continue to embrace asceticism.

The Occult Compendium

I can provide no singular method by which the Satanist may deprogram themselves- in this day and age we realize that psychology is not as we have been told in the past, with cookie-cutter people with virtually the same modus operandi and the same desires and goals on a psychic level; instead, we are left realizing that upbringing and genetics are fully mixed and create a plethora of individuals each with slightly different makeups of self, in which what works for one person may be utterly powerless in the life of another.

However, there are some concrete steps which I have personally observed working in the lives of the largest proportion of people I have taught them to, and it is through this process that I have attempted to help as many people overcome false guilt and fear wherever such help is requested. The first step is fairly simplistic, and requires a conscientious renunciation of the past system once enjoined, normally christianity or islam, and to a lesser extent certain branches, offshoots, or other groups associated with abrahamism (of note is that only very rarely do such negative feelings pervade the eastern traditions such as hinduism, although some groups surely have similar superstitions.)

The Occult Compendium

Only when the former religion is utterly renounced can the next steps be useful; if the individual merely stops going to church, or reading the bible, but still inside remains christian, or if they stop going to their mosque but still believe in allah, the following process will have no effect on them, or might disastrously have the opposite effect, as their inner voice (a sociologically programmed consciousness, not an absolutist conscience like a guardian angel) convinces them they are in danger, making them all that much more fervent.

Upon renunciation, an individual is left with a sort of psychological wound which if not properly treated can cause them immense psychological harm; we see this no better than in those who lose faith in their god and then wander through life feeling unfulfilled- I theorize that part of this is due to the introduction of religion into ones' life often during childhood, which is often a time of joy and relaxation, while on the flipside there are other children directly abused by religious families, teachers, or friends, which causes even more trauma to the young mind, especially when it comes frocked and carrying a "holy" book. To heal this wound, there are some concrete steps a

The Occult Compendium

person can take.

My first suggestion to people is often that they attempt to learn; religiosity (understood as dogmatic, prescribed-ritualistic thinking, as opposed to just 'spirituality' which is usually helpful and positive) tends to decline with education, regardless of what religious group we happen to observe; a person with a curious mind who questions things and wishes to investigate them often has little time for the dogma of others which they peddle as some sort of absolute truth. Some fields, additionally, are more valuable than others when it comes to replacing fear and guilt with curiosity, logic, reason, or even outright non-religious mysticism, I found my own study of anthropology was instrumental in allowing my mind to concoct the kind of philosophical materials to allow me to write, let alone to reason my way through such complicated issues within theology.

Anthropology aside, some other fields offer infinite potential; philosophy, logic, comparative religion, history, all of these can aid the mind; it is an open question as to whether the more abstract sciences and mathematics are of use in this goal, although I surmise they possibly could be-

The Occult Compendium

for a mind filled with the pure logic of mathematics too has little time for prescribed dogma.

Learning in this manner does not necessarily have to involve an actual academic pursuit- many people think that unless you happen to hold a degree you don't actually know anything about the subject, which couldn't be further from the truth. This is a myth, largely perpetuated by those with academic power who wish to continue to receive inordinate sums of money teaching people things they could learn more or less for free at their local library.

It suffices, for those who have no academic desires in this way, to study on the internet and (preferably also) from books; a great many philosophical works and historical texts can be found in even smaller libraries, with many more obscure texts and academic tracts available for anyone who wants them in paper form or for download online, all of which enhance the mind.

Upon beginning this process the individual ought not just to memorize information, but to practice applying and fuzing it- in essence, they must develop questions and then solve the questions for themselves, using their rational mind.

The Occult Compendium

Many people have a great deal of difficulty doing so (the main reason being the educational systems of the western world put almost all of their focus on memory, not application and cohesion) but practice makes perfect in this regard.

The Occult Compendium

REGARDING ANTON LAVEY AND THE CHURCH OF SATAN

Anton LaVey is remembered as the black pope, the father of what is now considered the modern Satanic movement- the fact that his teachings and beliefs have been perverted by others is now evident, particularly in the way people presume two things which LaVey himself likely would have recommended against.

The first mistake people make with Satanism is elevating LaVey to near deified status, assuming that whatever views he had and whatever "laws" for Satanists he made are unchanging and absolute- which would likely have amused the now deceased LaVey, who himself was probably intelligent enough to understand the evolutionary, almost darwinistic concept behind changes in cultural paradigms over time.

The second, and worse mistake, is in assuming that the foundational element of LaVey's founded "Church of Satan" is essentially an extension of his philosophy and beliefs, and that it serves the same purpose as it did when he

The Occult Compendium

was alive and in control of it. This is, however, not the case- as others who have held high positions in the Church of Satan have mentioned, the modern format of the Church of Satan is essentially a scam to extract money from rebellious teenagers and wannabe celebrities who believe giving their organization money for a little paper card announcing their membership will bring them power or fame or success.

LaVey was one part showman, one part philosopher, and one part conman- that he was a talented individual is beyond dispute- his musical abilities were quite good, and he was good at writing philosophical materials (although his only famous work is largely an adaptation of Ragnar Redbeard's *Might is Right.*) LaVey's main contribution to the world, at least in my own opinion, is helping bring back the essence of dark magick and occultism to a largely christian audience, that had even forsaken benign practices such as theosophy and meditation, thinking it an agent of Satan.

LaVey knew that he could make money by charging people for membership and ritual work as part of his organization- and herein lies something amusing, for while this type of con made it unlikely that a truly individualistic person would deign to pay him money to join, it was, on LaVey's end, perfectly Satanic, because he was not only doing what he wanted, but profiting from it!

It took the Church of Satan years to even bother updating their website, and I can personally attest to the nasty attitude of some of their upper level members and administrators- although I also believe that many of their members are faultless in joining them, because the organization has misrepresented itself to the public- not directly (lest their venture become dubiously legal) but indirectly, retaining the shadowy, mysterious form that LaVey left it in, while remaining an entirely above-board business that specializes in selling paper cards which anyone could print out on their own from a pirated blank, leaving their friends and family none the wiser.

It seems that a fairly large number of individuals within the upper levels of the Church of Satan consider any self-proclaimed Satanist outside of their membership to be illegitimate; for a long time I took this as a sign that they were continuing LaVey's somewhat conman money venture, but upon further review it seems likely that part of this is an effort to prevent lawsuits by outsiders who may try to claim

The Occult Compendium

Satanism as a defense in criminal proceedings (IE, "the cult told me to kill for Satan.")

Here we need to understand that LaVey himself largely gave up representing himself to the public by the middle of the 1980s and put his daughter Zeena in charge of most media appearances, often alongside her husband, Nikolas Schreck, who was not a member of the Church of Satan itself, but was involved with its proceedings and, through his eventual marriage to Zeena, was Anton Lavey's son in law. Zeena eventually left the Church in order to pursue membership within the Temple of Set, and later founded her own order, the Sethian Liberation Movement.

The more talented members of the Church of Satan, and the more talented people associated with it, in the modern age, have mostly abandoned it or renounced membership- from LaVey's daughter, to his apparent friend Boyd Rice (who, like LaVey himself, has produced a large quantity of music) to others who once flirted with the Church, or gained honorary membership- additionally, because of the Satanic Panic, many talented members that are active today probably do not publicly disclose membership.

The Occult Compendium

However, the Church of Satan that exists today is not the same as the one which existed when LaVey was alive- the Black House of San Francisco has been demolished, and they work now mainly out of an administrative building in New York- what was once a home endeavor by a theatrically inclined LaVey has become more of a business than a form of entertainment- few can argue that LaVey himself took great amusement when he declared the age of the cross to be over, subsequently drawing the ire of millions of christians; for remember, around that time period the western world was solidly religious- even religious groups which are now generally tolerated by the christian majority such as hinduism or mormonism were severely opposed and considered heretical until the 1990s, by which time LaVey was already deceased.

It would be philosophically strange for a group which evolved with the ethos of individuality to then attempt to claim that those outside of its membership are not part of that same philosophy, by virtue of a decision not to join, while still adhering to the same basic philosophy.

It seems likely that Anton LaVey most likely wished

The Occult Compendium

Satanism to be something more than what it turned out to be. Despite claims to the contrary by those "close" to LaVey (including dozens of hangers-on that likely only spoke with him rarely and about frivolous matters) I cannot myself imagine that even he himself merely meant it to be a scam. While some people who recognize the modern Church of Satan to be largely an effort to make money and mock christians put the blame squarely on Anton LaVey, it might be more appropriate to blame him only because he failed to put in place an organizational capacity capable of perpetuating the ideology effectively; it is quite possible he planned to do so but was taken by death before he was able to do so, and by that time he mostly allowed others to lead and represent his organization.

Indeed, even the christians who see a picture of LaVey and get tingles up and down their spine might have the right idea when they proclaim that LaVey had a sort of demonic force around him. Whether or not you believe in literal demons, LaVey did have a sort of aura around him able to influence others, although I myself consider this far more likely the result of charisma and perhaps a possible familiarity with theosophy and perhaps hypnosis or other fields of pseudoscience- whatever the case, however, for his

The Occult Compendium

attractiveness towards others, it is clear that he was able at the least to influence several major celebrities during his lifetime, as well as hordes of less well known individuals, and he did seem to surround himself with those involved with or interested in the occult.

I find myself struggling actually, with the topic of Anton LaVey; one part of me wants to excoriate him utterly for lacking the foresight to build a Satanic system of substantial psychological value, while the other part wishes to believe that he was merely self assured in his work and realized or at least believed that someone else would finish or expand upon it even if he died; if the christians are correct and he was secretly involved with actual mysticism it's quite possible he predicted this would be the case, but there is no definitive evidence that he went beyond showmanship and illusion in his study, suggesting that he had at most a modest understanding of symbolism and the arcane.

Even if we assume LaVey was utterly atheistic (as the organization either was or at least currently is) and never cared about his own work beyond its capacity to generate a profit, we can still fault the modern Church of Satan for not implementing any form of plan designed to expand beyond

The Occult Compendium

word of mouth; which makes for a very exciting and "secretive" group that nonetheless, eventually, will be shoved into obscurity- in fact, because the COS itself does so little other groups with essentially the same or similar ideologies have sprung up all across the western world, almost all of which are more publicly visible and active, and some of which are quickly rising in prominence as they grow in size- a proposed occultist LaVey likely foresaw this and laughed, realizing he needed only to write a book and conduct a few black masses before the idea itself would take root, slowly growing even after his corpse froze in the soil.

Of course, he himself was largely eclipsed in the 1980s and beyond by others who took a more activist approach towards Satanism, devil worship, the occult, and other related fields of study and other related spiritual movements; Wicca is growing so quickly in clout that within a few decades it may be a substantial world religious force, paganism is making a comeback particularly with Hellenism and Odinism growing swiftly, and occultism is reaching an ever more vast audience as well.

In this period of time LaVey might have been astonished to find that those he associated with had become more culturally prominent than he was simply by appearing more publicly visible, especially his cohort Aquino and the Setian movement, best illustrated by the conspicuous absence of LaVey during Geraldo Rivera's well meaning but utterly hilarious "Devil Worship, Exposing Satan's Underground" special, one of several during the Satanic Panic era which generated enormous interest and, later on, enormous embarrassment for the media at large. While Anton himself was absent, his own daughter, Zeena appeared alongside Aquino at this time- and although the two together were given precious little time to refute the general consensus of the "documentary" itself (namely that occultists and Satanists were trying to recruit children and were regularly sacrificing humans to the devil) they were at least present, with even Ozzy Osbourne himself making a guest appearance, apparently confused at the claims being made regarding heavy metal and rock.

By that time LaVey himself was mostly retired to private life and continued only in a figurehead fashion, having apparently lost interest in public dialogue- this led to the necessity of others representing the "church" and resulted in various figures questioning why Anton was not being exposed to public scrutiny.

The Occult Compendium

A REFERENDUM ON VARIOUS THEISTIC SATANISTS

Here we must now discuss a particularly sticky issue and one which constantly redirects the ire of both atheistic and theistic Satanic groups away from the real target (which as always are the abrahamists and certain political and social forces which try to suppress alternative ideologies) and at one another- these problems have been exacerbated by misunderstandings on both sides towards the other, as well as likely deliberate attacks by abrahamists themselves, in order to cause infighting and debates to rage. The law enforcement community has long clung to 1980s era manuscripts regarding Satanism, and amusingly continue to determine, whenever ritual murder is suspected, what grimoire the group is reading from, ignoring groups which don't use such texts or even regard them as hilariously silly.

Theistic Satanism, is not monolithic (much like atheistic Satanism, although some hold the misguided belief that it is) but is broken down into multiple philosophical and occult groups, as well as into various physical bodies which sometimes have their own teachings separate from the

The Occult Compendium

others- groups which may be as small as two or three members, or might number in the hundreds. Some theistic Satanists see Satan as more of a cosmic energy or force, while others see a literal, sometimes even physical being possessed of intelligence and volition. Some theistic Satanists are nihilistic or practice a sort of self destructive path, believing that this will unite them with this primordial force of chaos and darkness, while others take up a more romanticist line towards Satan whether being or force or ideology, and consider it positive, while regarding other deities as negative or even malevolent.

There are other groups, such as Joy of Satan, which regard Satan as a sort of alien or creature from another world- something which has some historical truth to it, since the modern story of the serpent of genesis (modern comparatively, that is) is at least loosely based on Sumerian writings that date to centuries before any fragment of the old testament was written- to them, Satan is Enki, a sort of Promethean liberation figure, which may return to Earth in the future; Seth from Egypt might be seen as a loose extension of this same figure as well.

In any case, however, an unfortunate amount of

The Occult Compendium

fighting has been seen between each of these groups and one another, as well as with LaVeyyan Satanists, often as members of the Church of Satan (which doesn't help the situation by heaping abuse on theistic Satanists using terms like "occultnics" to describe them.)

That all of the above, as well as LaVeyyan Satanism, alongside wicca and paganism, are all technically on the same side and fighting for similar goals seems to have escaped the attention of both the members of these groups as well as the abrahamists- we could also lump in nonreligious forces such as the "vampire" communities of the world (which range from blood drinking sanguinarians to "psychic" vampies as well as roleplay communities) as well as those who practice certain new age philosophies, which are more similar to the Enki-awaiting theistic Satanists than most other schools.

If the enemy of my enemy is my friend, then surely the snide remarks and disdain, if not outright hostility, which certain members of all of these groups show towards one another, cannot be anything other than fuel for a fire which doesn't need to be burning. There are many similarities between Satanic and other associated groups, far more than there are differences.

The Occult Compendium

I can't think of any group even loosely associated with this branch of philosophy that doesn't benefit from if not outright preach an individualistic mindset and a conscientious approach to spirituality in general; none of these groups, except for certain cults which have only the most tenuous attachment to Satanism, attempt to stomp out their members' individual endeavors in favor of a highly organized and somewhat abrahamist-style approach.

To the theistic Satanist, often, Satan is a force of liberation or a symbol of individual power and ability, or a being concerned with warring against a god that only a fool would consider anything other than tyrannical. In these cases, and seeing the behavior of the christians and islamists and jews against people within Satanism, wicca, paganism, and other groups, can we believe even for a moment that these people and their gods, whether real or imagined, are "good" or virtuous?

Regardless of the ultimate goal of the specific ideology, the general notion that the right hand path with its guilt slavery and psychological disease is negative and untrustworthy remains more or less intact, with a degree of

The Occult Compendium

flexibility consequently aligned only to each individual groups' veneration of an actual deity or force, or lack thereof. The philosophical Satanist is concerned mostly with liberating the mind and body, other groups might be concerned with liberating the planet of degrading forces (primitivism or naturism) or liberating the cosmos from an evil god (as is the case with some theistic Satanists.)

The Occult Compendium

ARCHETYPES OF SATAN

The topic at hand here is simply *what or who is Satan?* This can be a confusing topic, which I have spoken to others about and attempted in some way to resolve, both in my own mind and for others- while the specific roots of this being as an archetype (and there are multiple archetypes) are not always completely known, it is possible to look through older pagan religions and to a few linguistic terms and derive what we can say is at least the most close-to-truth definition of Satan.

To understand this being we first have to differentiate between Satan, Lucifer, the Devil, and other related beings, and then we have to fully study the archetypes used during different time periods to describe this being in its three major and several minor forms- entire works could be written solely on the topic of the appearance and characteristics of the Prince of Darkness, but here it will suffice to include a more broad overview in a single chapter, so as not to overwhelm this work with academic terms.

First, let us consider the being called Lucifer- this

The Occult Compendium

word, Lucifer, itself, is not a proper noun in its original Latin- indeed, while christians today treat this as a name for the being also called Satan, not only are these two beings essentially different characters altogether, the word itself is misused in the most pathological of ways.

The word Lucifer itself, is a Latin term merely meaning "bearer of light" or "morning star" (Venus) depending on who you ask, or literally "something which is glowing or giving off light within the visible spectrum"- the individuals translating the bible seem not to have understood this, and translated (in the new testament) the original Greek term *phosphoros* to *Lucifer* as a proper noun, apparently not realizing that phosphoros, which has literally an identical meaning to lucifer, is not a proper noun, but a characteristic which can apply to an individual, an inanimate object, or be used as a metaphor in either case.

The confusion continues because Lucifer can also refer to the literal morning star (giver of light) as either the planet Venus or any deity or being ascribed to it or its house in the heavens.

In the case of the bible, use of the term Lucifer

The Occult Compendium

(which doesn't even always appear in modern translations) can refer to the Devil, Jesus, or other figures or concepts almost interchangeably- I would list here several verses in which it appears, but it would require a review of many translations, which differ on the subject, with some more honestly using the term in its original form, and other, far less accurate translations (such as the dishonestly applied but often applauded King James Version) using it mainly as a term to denote it is speaking about Satan.

We then have to review the Devil himself- the "old serpent" of revelation, in all of his wonder and glory and supposed power in the world; the most reviled figure in all of antiquity and modernity, which so many people so fear and reject.

This being, different from the often misunderstood Lucifer, is best seen as a loose adaptation of ancient pagan deities; here we need to understand that the Jews who first developed this concept were henotheists, meaning that while they believed that the deities and beings worshiped or believed in by other cultures were real, they chose their own specific deity, kept it separate, and largely felt that all foreign gods and beings were evil or at least not to be worshiped by

The Occult Compendium

their own population- oddly, after wandering the desert suffering for many years, the bible tells us that Moses disappeared into the mountains for an extended period of time, after which the hebrews magically accrued enough gold to smelt a large calf statue, which they subsequently worshiped as pagans, angering both Moses and Jehovah- that this is fantastic and unlikely is clear, but it makes at least some sense considering the pagans already had various cattle gods.

The modern christian seems to forget this henotheistic origin of their religion, seemingly oblivious to the fact that the earliest incarnation of the Devil seems to have been as a remarkably similar being to certain pagan beings (Baal, or the plural sometimes used, "Baal's") including Beelzebub.

That the culturally egotistical and henotheistic Jews also borrowed, seemingly, large elements from Sumerian lore during their time spent near and in Babylon, forming parts of the old testament, is virtually beyond dispute- the Epic of Gilgamesh and other Sumerian writings predate the first Jewish texts by many centuries, yet tell remarkably similar stories- and if not for the bible itself mentioning the

The Occult Compendium

captivity in Babylon it might have been impossible to make a true connection between the two cultures. Here we have a Devil, which evolved from their primitive understanding of rituals and beings they would have found evil or at least frightening, building it into a negative being to be avoided- this being was then absorbed into the Jewish pantheon of lesser beings and given the purpose of their gods trickster angel, which many extrabiblical tales refer to as mischievous, but not necessarily an out and out malevolent being, somewhat along the lines of a foul mouthed, gambling poltergeist that tries to convince people to sin.

The Occult Compendium

THE EVILS OF ABRAHAMISM

Now it is time to expose once and for all the vile and evil ways of the abrahamist- those schools of religious thought that link themselves mythically with this figure of Abraham, who may or may not have even existed or, like jesus, might be mostly anecdotal stories applied to a central figure of far less importance. Because it is the oldest of the three groups, we will begin first with the evils of the Jews, with their tyrant god- keeping in mind the whole time as we must, that criticism of Judaism, or of Israel, do not connote antisemitism, but rather legitimate criticism as it may be applied to any other group of people or their spirituality.

When we criticize these groups as we must, it is worth noting that because all are fractured into many smaller groups or sects, that criticism does not necessarily apply equally to them all- if we pointed out the homophobic bigotry of the christian population, we would then have to admit that there are christian churches that do not care about the issue and do not prescribe intolerance or violence towards homosexuals, just as there are islamists who do not advocate the beheading of apostates.

The Occult Compendium

The bipolarity of the jewish creed may best be seen when we compare the nation of Israel (Mandatory Palestine, when it was run by the British until the mid 1900s) and its policies with the ideas and policies of jewish individuals living elsewhere. The nation of Israel is a racially homogeneous (or nearly so) state, allowed to perpetuate bigotry towards nonjewish individuals, holding immigrants without trial, sterilizing minorities, and deporting asylum seekers. In the rest of the world, jewish individuals have been at the forefront of attempts to integrate societies, mixing them together until all that is left is a confused population with no actual culture. Oddly, Israel itself has no true culture, considering most of the people in charge there are Eastern Europeans by race and atheists by religion; something which has vexed the orthodox judaists, who have protested the very existence of this state many times in the past.

Israeli policy is to create and maintain a solely jewish state, along ethnic and religious lines, something which Israeli-backed groups such as AIPAC would deeply oppose if it were applied in a white or asian nation- the militarism of Israel towards all neighbors who do not bend over

The Occult Compendium

backwards for it has done more to destabilize the region than any war of aggression by the west could ever hope to accomplish.

In fact, the same imperialism, nationalism, racism, and general bigotry denounced in the west, and the rise of, within academic circles, attempts to force the youth to "appreciate" foreigners in their midst, is roughly opposite everything Israel has become- a small, backwards state run by a combination of racial fanatics and radically warmongering political groups, to the point where even embattled war "hero" Ariel Sharon was eventually seen as too moderate for pledging to work towards the creation of an independent Palestinian state.

This is not to implicate all Jewish individuals in these things- Judaism itself is a root from which the far worse christian and islamic branches divided, but the Orrthodoxy, other than the usual superstition, at least has the decency to oppose zionism, while the corpus of Jewish individuals in the western world no longer care to support either orthodox religious zeal or extremists- however, the same orthodoxy that will verbally assault Israeli policy also endorses the practice of circumcision- which contrary to popular belief

The Occult Compendium

has no medical value as a procedure and is at best a violation of the religious liberty of children the world over.

And these same individuals, joined even by Jews who do not care about Judaism but enjoy their cultural heritage, will cry antisemitism at anyone who suggests that the right of a child to retain full sexual function- a child that most often isn't even old enough to verbalize- trumps the superstitious rituals thereof.

Here begins the stupidity of the christians as well- for these christians will form ranks immediately to defend what they consider "gods chosen people" (showing the racism of their evil god) even when they reside in nations which were founded on secular law and plurality. These same christians would light the torches and grab the pitchforks, so to speak, were a religious body to arise and persist in any western nation, which taught that it was part of some obscure cultural heritage to otherwise modify the human body- which has resulted in a bizarre situation where christians will oppose female circumcision as it is performed by certain islamic sects, while supporting male circumcision, which is essentially the same thing, although they will claim otherwise.

The Occult Compendium

And these same christians and jews delight in mentioning repeatedly that culture has become somehow degraded and "bad" despite helping it to become this way- in a true reference to Friederich Nieszche, whose famous words "The christian resolution to find the world ugly and bad has made the world ugly and bad" ring true especially in the modern age.

The true horror, however, of all forms of abrahamism, is their tendency to encourage parents and clergy alike to browbeat young individuals who aren't even yet at fully functioning mental levels, into retaining a sort of guilt and fear, so that they do not leave the religion, or so that if they do eventually leave it, they leave it in an emotionally unstable state ensuring that for the rest of their life, in many cases, they worry about their own decision. These religions do not make good leaders, they make good manipulators, and they do not allow individualism, as they teach that thinking for oneself is in some way evil or Satanic. (On this latter point, at least, they have a little truth- for Satanism is able to teach that which abrahamism cannot.)

The Occult Compendium

Anyone who has traveled to the southern states within the USA has seen the vast churches that have been constructed, often with money that was siphoned from the very poor, little by little, and invested in holdings designed to make even more income; the Vatican famously owns a publishing house that produces none other than LaVey's "Satanic Bible" and more recently even acquired a building in Rome that to this day, it is said, still includes a men's bathhouse where gay activity is said to be commonplace- all while denouncing these same things in public, hoping the laypeople do not find out about their often criminal activities.

Nothing, however, is more hideous within any christian body, than a preacher ranting, fiery-eyed at a crowd of tongue-speaking fanatic followers, about the importance of humility and immaterialism, while standing before a ten foot tall, gold-covered cross, in a building worth tens of millions of dollars, that otherwise could have been given to the poor or the orphans and widows as their own messiah commanded- and these same idiotic followers, that obviously haven't even studied their own bible, will then take to the streets to tell others how sinful they are, and how

The Occult Compendium

they're headed to eternal perdition.

Here I will say: were their savior actually real, and not a partially mythological story based on a dead ascetic or perhaps Appolonius of Tyana depending on who you ask, then this jesus that they worship would slit their throats, send them to Hell forever, and laugh as he burns their churches to the ground. The megachurch pastors and the bishops in soaring cathedrals will never admit this to be true, in typical fashion, but will sit and absorb millions of dollars in tax free cash from impoverished people whose own feelings of guilt that the church itself created keep them paying up at the offering plate.

There are also examples where christian clergy of various backgrounds have been so directly implicated in hypocrisy that it is surprising anyone even takes them seriously, such as our old friend Ted Haggard, a famous evangelist minister who spent years preaching that homosexuality was sinful and homosexuals capable of being "cured" by therapy. Subsequently, this man was implicated in a scandal involving another man and drug use. This effectively ended his ministry, until years later when he began anew, with a new flock that was either oblivious to his

The Occult Compendium

past or didn't care because he was charismatic.

Satanists especially have to deal with the regressive minds of the christian. Many times have we all heard "how can you worship Satan and not believe in God?" Many times we have all heard "I pray to jesus for your soul" and a million permutations of this basic statement. When a Satanist attempts to tell the christian that Satanism (at least philosophical Satanism) has nothing to do with devil worship, they dwell obsessively on Satanism as a title- the only way to explain this phenomenon to them seems to be to mention Platonism and ask them if it regards the worship of Plato as a deity.

Many of these individuals are not to blame- their views have been fed to them for a long time, sometimes since birth, and for a christian raised in an evangelical home, even becoming a liberal christian or agnostic is quite a feat. The level of brainwashing experienced even by non-evangelical christians at a young age makes the attempts of MK-Ultra or the KGB or Gestapo seem tame by comparison. The real threat, here, are the leaders of the christian movement and its various offshoots, as well as sometimes well-meaning but utterly delusional parents who

The Occult Compendium

will regularly beat their children for imagined sins. This may explain why a plurality of all serial killers and lunatics in the western world were raised in religiously christian families.

Even worse than the lies and hypocrisy of christianity, if such a thing is even possible, are the lies and hypocrisy of islam- a religion for which some sects even enshrine lies told to nonbelievers (termed taqqiya) as tolerated or even positive behavior- and from beheading apostates (those who, born muslim, have left islam) to stoning adulterers, even "moderate" islamists make the evangelical christians look like model citizens.

I have spoken to numerous individuals from the Middle East, and I can say with certainty that a large number of individuals there, particularly teenagers and females, are not religious, and only call themselves islamic out of fear of being killed should they fail to exhibit what their cultures deem normal islamic behavior. This phenomenon roughly mimics pre-internet western christianity, where even utterly atheistic or even antitheistic individuals would continue attending worship services out of a fear of being beaten in the street, or shunned by their family, should they publicly disclose their doubt in faith. Islam is best understood as

The Occult Compendium

largely the ravings of a medieval-era madman, who used his manipulative abilities to rise up from poverty into a position of tribal power.

The fanatic islamists often use the internet in an attempt to indoctrinate westerners into their cult- thankfully, the majority of those foolish enough to convert end up leaving islam fairly quickly, but whenever conversion takes place, it involves a fanatic using taqqiya- for a liberal muslim would have no reason to try and convert others, and certain groups such as the Salafi islamists frown upon the use of taqqiya.

The Occult Compendium

CHAPTER VIII

Occult Resources

It is important, I believe, to give here a fairly complete list of various groups associated with, or a direct part of, the Satanic movement, along with a general summary of any information I can glean regarding their activities and so forth. I do not intend here to give any support or criticism to such groups, as I am not a member of any of them, and represent, mostly, only myself and those directly under my wing which I counsel regarding such issues.

Not all of these groups are Satanic, some are occult or pagan, and others merely contain teachings, texts, or other phenomena which give it some link to Satanism, whether it be through environmental activism or libertarianism. Of special note here, is that many websites dedicated to Satanic teaching that are listed on some compilational pages are expired and inactive or else have not been updated in some time and are glitchy- in the post-social media era, some sites withered and others expanded

The Occult Compendium

substantially. Indeed, there are thousands of websites and organizations that could be listed here, but actually finding even a fraction of them would take inordinate effort, and thus some of the more prominent names appear here; others are forthcoming to anyone willing to research the topic.

CHURCH OF SATAN: Obviously the best known Satanic movement in the world, it's administrative headquarters is located in Poughkeepsie, New York, and they operate a substantially active website, although there are fanpages run by those who aren't even in the church itself that also receive substantial traffic.

TEMPLE OF SET: Michael Aquino's organization, identifying the ancient Egyptian figure of Set (sometimes Seth) as being either the original Satan or another term for the same being. The organization is administrated out of San Francisco.

SETHIAN LIBERATION MOVEMENT: A Sethian order headed by Zeena Schreck, daughter of Anton LaVey and former priestess in the Temple of Set; its contact is through Berlin, Germany. This particular movement is not

The Occult Compendium

the same as Aquino's Temple of Set, although some are confused and erroneously believe this to be the case.

THE SATANIC TEMPLE: A now-infamous New York based Satanic group which rose to prominence after crowdfunding money to build a statue of Baphomet and have it installed next to a ten commandments monument in Oklahoma. The group is active and growing.

CULT OF LILITH: A possibly defunct movement regarding nihilism and demonolatry, identifying the figure of Lilith as a sort of primordial chaos mother that once had at least one active website and blog as well as a manifesto expounding the virtue of chaos over order.

BROTHERHOOD OF SATAN: Based in Georgia, seemingly a web-only organization with a postal location claiming to conduct actual occult rituals (differentiating it from atheistic orders and groups such as the Church of Satan.)

THE BLACK ORDER: A presumably defunct pagan and aryan supremacist order once run out of New Zealand; original copies of "Flaming Sword" (their monthly

The Occult Compendium

bulletin) exist but only a few issues seem available for review.

THE ODINIST FELLOWSHIP: Pagan revival group from England (post out of London) which claims Odinism as the original and true religion of England and conducts various education and outreach.

THE ASATRU ALLIANCE: Payson Arizona-based asatru organization stressing the importance of norse revivalism.

AMERICAN ASATRU ASSOCIATION: Another asatru order, mostly involved, seemingly, with perpetuating the ways of heathenism and prechristian tribal naturism. Their website lists numerous contacts with smaller, internalized asatru orders and groups throughout the US as well as South Africa and Chile.

THEOSOPHICAL SOCIETY: A theosophical order dedicated to various scientific (and pseudoscientific) studies, various fields of the humanities, and to peripherally occult topics. Its headquarters are located in Adyar, within Chennai, India.

The Occult Compendium

THE ROSICRUCIAN FELLOWSHIP: A mystery school and philosophical order loosely associated with protestant christianity, but with templar overtones and various supposedly occult connections. Based out of Oceanside California.

ASTARA: A new age, somewhat UFO related movement from which numerous texts from the 1960s through the present era are extant dealing with everything from prophecy to light work to alien life forms. It is based out of Rancho Cucamonga, California.

UNITED SATANIC EMPIRE: Based in the Southern US, an atheistic Satanic order that maintained a website and multiple youtube channels but which appears to be partially defunct, one member being expelled and another becoming ill; their website appears to be active, however.

SINAGOGUE OF SATAN: A theistic Satanic order which may or may not be currently active; their website lists Satan as the reverse, or negation of, the jewish Yahweh.

The Occult Compendium

ORDER OF PHOSPHORUS: A Luciferian initiatory order teaching self realization and consciousness transformation.

SOCIETY OF THE ONYX STAR: Branch of the First Church of Satan, which appears active and maintains a members-only board.

JOY OF SATAN: A large community of theistic Satanists and occultists which maintain both a website and a well trafficked yahoo group online- their philosophy recognizes Satan and other cosmic entities as extra terrestrial beings and has substantial outreach to the internet world- the forum contains many topics, notably regarding meditation and evocation.

REFORMED CHURCH OF SATAN: A positive-minded Satanic movement which incorporates some material from other paths; it maintains an active presence on Facebook but their website appears offline.

WICCAN TOGETHER: An online community dedicated to wicca with a very large current presence; finding individual covens is somewhat difficult (especially as

The Occult Compendium

some do not openly proclaim their own existence and may contain few members.) As such, most wiccan material is clustered on this and similar sites geared towards meetups and information sharing.

WITCHVOX: Another online wiccan (and pagan) community of similar size and traffic- it also contains articles pertaining to the topic of witchcraft.

PAGAN FEDERATION: An organization and website dedicated to connecting wiccans and pagans from across the globe and performing various ministering and interfaith outreach; most of its content is members-only.

THE ROWAN TREE CHURCH: A movement based in Kirkland, Washington, which stresses connectedness to the Earth and the teaching of the craft of magick. It appears to be active. This particular church also makes use of Buddhist and Native folklore and craft.

THE CORRELLIAN TRADITION: A Correllian wiccan movement that may be inactive, as evidenced by errors on their website. However, the site contains members-only content and that partition may be active.

The Occult Compendium

In addition to all listed groups and movements there remain many millions of individual and group practitioners of Satanism, Paganism, Wicca, and all forms of the occult, many of which closet their beliefs and may not publicly proclaim themselves members of such orders and temples.

CPSIA information can be obtained
at www.ICGtesting.com
Printed in the USA
BVHW040819091118
532660BV00005B/53/P